# Program Monitoring and Visualization

**Springer**
*New York*
*Berlin*
*Heidelberg*
*Barcelona*
*Hong Kong*
*London*
*Milan*
*Paris*
*Singapore*
*Tokyo*

Clinton L. Jeffery

# Program Monitoring and Visualization

## An Exploratory Approach

**With 46 Illustrations**

 Springer

Clinton Jeffery
Department of Computer Science
University of Nevada, Las Vegas
Las Vegas, NV 89154-4019

Library of Congress Cataloging-in-Publication Data
Jeffery, Clinton L.
     Program monitoring and visualization : an exploratory approach
/ Clinton L. Jeffery.
       p.   cm.
     Includes bibliographical references and index.

     ISBN-13: 978-1-4612-7438-4        e-ISBN-13: 978-1-4612-2160-9
     DOI: 10.1007/978-1-4612-2160-9


     1. Visual programming (Computer science)   2. Software engineering.
I. Title.
     QA76.65.J45   1999
     005.1´18—dc21                                         98-31161

Printed on acid-free paper.


© 1999 Springer-Verlag New York, Inc.
Softcover reprint of the hardcover 1st edition 1999

Production managed by Steven Pisano; manufacturing supervised by Nancy Wu.
Photocomposed pages prepared from the author's LaTeX files.



9 8 7 6 5 4 3 2 1

ISBN-13: 978-1-4612-7438-4  Springer-Verlag  New York  Berlin  Heidelberg   SPIN 10696073

# Preface

Program visualization is a branch of software visualization, an emerging software engineering discipline. Program visualization uses program execution monitors to improve our understanding of program runtime behavior. This contrasts with other forms of software visualization such as the animation of individual algorithms for educational purposes, or the visualization of data stored in files.

Program visualization tools are used in a variety of important applications such as debugging, performance tuning, and the study of algorithms. Unfortunately, progress in this area of systems software has been slow due to the difficulty of the task of writing execution monitors.

In high-level programming languages, the task of writing execution monitors is made more complex by features such as nontraditional control flow and complex semantics. Additionally, in many languages such as Visual Basic, Java, REXX, Perl, or the Icon programming language, a significant part of the execution behavior that monitors need to observe occurs in the language virtual machine and runtime system rather than the source code of the monitored program.

Icon is an innovative, very high-level language developed at the University of Arizona. It is best suited to rapid prototyping and experimental programs, situations where programmer time is precious. This book presents a framework for monitoring Icon programs. The framework is organized by a monitor architecture called Alamo [37], and allows rapid development of execution monitors in the Icon language itself. This allows the benefits of the Icon language to extend to the task of writing visualization tools. Additionally, the framework gives monitors full source-level access to the target program with which to gather and process execution information, without intrusive modification to the target executable. In addition, the framework supports the monitoring of implicit runtime system behavior crucial to program understanding.

In order to demonstrate its practicality, the framework has been used to implement a collection of program visualization tools. Program visualization provides graphical feedback about program execution that allows human beings to deal with volumes of data more effectively than textual techniques. Ideally, the user specifies program execution controls in such tools directly in the graphics used to visualize execution, employing the same visual language that is used to render the output. Some monitors that exhibit this characteristic are presented.

This book is organized into four parts. Part I is an overview of execution monitoring and program visualization and a survey of the state of the art in the field. Part II presents the Alamo monitor architecture and the framework that Alamo provides for monitoring Icon programs. Alamo was developed in order to facilitate the construction of visualization tools. Part III demonstrates the utility of the framework with code and screen images for a series of example visualization tools that observe many kinds of execution behavior. Part IV discusses the use of program visualization tools in a practical programming environment; relevant issues include tool integration as well as the performance of collections of monitors executing on real programs. Following Part IV is a collection of appendices including some detailed program examples and a description of the implementation of the monitoring framework.

# Acknowledgments

Ralph Griswold directed the doctoral work from which this book sprang. Committee members Rick Snodgrass and Mary Bailey provided valuable input on the early form and content of this book; I am very grateful to them for their detailed readings and comments. Norm Hutchinson taught me how to develop large software systems.

Some of the example execution monitors in this book were written by Wenyi Zhou, Kevin Templer, Ralph Griswold, and Gregg Townsend. Ralph Griswold and Gregg Townsend did most of the instrumentation of the Icon runtime system. Ken Walker also contributed to the instrumentation. The cone tree images were programmed in OpenGL by Michael Brazell in his tree visualizer for the Alamo C framework.

Valuable experience with the Icon framework was gained with the help of numerous computer scientists at the University of Arizona such as Darren Merrill, Mary Cameron, Jon Lipp, Nick Kline, Song Liang, and Kevin Devries. My academic big brother Steve Wampler has also made many valuable comments. Students at UT San Antonio have also written fascinating monitors or implemented useful visualization aids, including Thanawat Lertpradist, Laura Connor, Anthony Jones, Khan Mai, and Niem Tang.

Steven Pisano, Fred Bartlett, and the rest of the staff at Springer-Verlag provided excellent and detailed editing and technical assistance with the preparation of this manuscript, which was done by the author in LaTeX.

This work was supported in part by the National Science Foundation under Grants CCR-8713690, CCR-9409082, and CDA-9633299, and a grant from the AT&T Research Foundation.

Las Vegas, June 1999                                    Clinton L. Jeffery

# Contents

# Part I

# Fundamental Concepts

Part II

# Fundamental Concepts

# 1

# Introduction

Monitoring and visualizing the dynamic behavior of programs is a major area of research that has not been fully explored. The motivation for this research is a need for better tools to aid in the understanding of dynamic aspects of program behavior during various phases of the software life cycle, including debugging, performance tuning, and maintenance.

This book presents Alamo [37], a software architecture for monitoring the execution of programs that makes it easy to write a broad assortment of monitors, especially program visualization tools. After presenting the architecture itself, the book illustrates the capture and visualization of a wide range of program behaviors by presenting code fragments and example screen images.

The Alamo architecture is language-independent. Alamo was first implemented in a framework for monitoring programs written in the Icon programming language [28]. Icon is an ideal tool for exploring and developing research ideas. The examples in this book are written in Icon and tested using that framework. The success of the Icon implementation lead to grant support and a second implementation for a more mainstream compiled language, ANSI C. When it is mature, the Alamo C framework will provide a natural migration path for the best ideas discovered using the Icon framework.

This chapter describes software development tasks that motivate the development of visualization tools and defines a class of programs called execution monitors that aid our understanding of program behavior. The chapter concludes with an overview of the rest of the book and its contribution to the field of execution monitoring.

## 1.1  Understanding Program Behavior

Program-understanding is a very general topic. Some program-understanding systems convey very specific information about a small portion of a program, such as the workings of a single algorithm. Others are concerned with explaining the role that a program or a collection of programs plays within a larger computational system. This book addresses a common problem in between these two extremes: understanding the workings of a single (possibly large) program.

People who are confronted by a need to understand a program usually have only two alternatives: studying the source code, or running the program to see what it does. Ideally, a program would be understandable using one or the other of these methods; in practice, reading source code is impractically cumbersome for many programs, and construction of test cases to explain program behavior is often a tedious and speculative undertaking. These difficulties motivate the development of special programs that are used to help explain the behavior of other programs.

Program-understanding systems are used in a variety of applications. The most common motive for program-understanding is *debugging*. Programs that produce incorrect output or fail to complete their execution due to bugs are prime candidates for tools that assist program developers and maintainers in program-understanding tasks. A *debugger* is a program designed specifically to help with the debugging process. General-purpose program-understanding tools are also used to assist in debugging.

A second major application of program-understanding systems is *performance tuning* or *performance debugging*. A correct, working program may be of limited usefulness if its performance is poor. Frequently, a program's authors or maintainers can improve execution speed by using different programming techniques or modifying the program's algorithms and data structures. By providing an accounting of which resources the program is using and which sections of code are primarily responsible, performance tuning systems can direct programmers' efforts to where they are most needed.

A third application of program-understanding is *software instruction* and *orientation*. The internal workings of a program may be of special interest to students learning important algorithms, data structures, or programming techniques; this situation frequently arises when learning a new language. People assigned to maintain or improve a program written by someone else similarly need to *orient* themselves as to its general operation. In both of these cases, the people involved may be entirely unfamiliar with the program source code, and can benefit from information provided by program understanding tools before consulting source code, or without referring to it at all.

In addition to these established uses for program-understanding systems, program-understanding tools can provide language implementors with valuable assistance in the task of *language implementation tuning*. Program-understanding tools that provide information about the execution of programs also directly or indirectly provide information about the language's implementation. This information can be used to improve performance or address problems in the implementation.

## 1.2     Types of Program-Understanding Tools

Programs that provide information about other programs can be separated into two main categories based on the kind of information they provide. *Static analysis tools* examine the program text and, in conjunction with knowledge of the language, provide information about a program that is true for all executions of that program independent of its input [15]. Compiler code optimizers, pretty printers, and syntax-directed editors frequently employ static analysis techniques.

In general, static information cannot explain program behavior because behavior depends on input data in addition to the program text. For example, the number of times through a loop may depend on the size of an input file, or the execution path through a conditional statement may depend on interactive user input from a keyboard or mouse.

*Dynamic analysis tools* provide information about a specific program execution on a specific set of input data [15]. Since dynamic analysis involves extracting information from a running program rather than its source code, these tools pose implementation problems that are very different from those found in static analysis tools. Another name for a dynamic analysis tool is a *program execution monitor*. A program execution monitor is a program that monitors the execution of another program [53]. Program execution monitors complement static analysis tools and provide execution information that static tools cannot, such as details about the program's control flow, intermediate results that are computed, or depictions of internal data structures as the program runs. On the other hand, static aspects of a program such as variable names often provide context crucial to the understanding of execution behavior. Good dynamic analysis tools incorporate static information in support of dynamic information. Execution monitors include the source-level debuggers and profilers commonly bundled with compilers and available on many operating systems.

An execution monitor may either present information to the user as the program executes (immediate or *runtime* analysis), or it may present information at some later time such as after execution completes (*postmortem* analysis). Runtime analyzers provide immediate feedback and allow user direction of the kind and level of detail of the information monitored. In contrast, postmortem analyzers may perform extensive computations to condense the execution information and present it in a useful way. The two methods are not mutually exclusive.

Runtime analysis tools can further be categorized as *passive* or *interactive*. In a passive system, the tool presents information to the user, but the user has little control over the activity. In an interactive system, the user may have external control over what information is displayed, or even may be able to modify the computation being observed or the data being processed.

## 1.3    Scope of This Book

This book presents an architecture and framework that facilitate the development of new and experimental execution monitors, particularly interactive runtime analysis tools for very high-level sequential languages. It is not concerned with monitoring techniques for parallel, distributed, or realtime computing systems, although the monitoring of such systems does require effective sequential monitoring techniques.

This book discusses execution monitors within a well-defined context: the Icon programming language. Icon is a high-level procedural language that descends primarily from SNOBOL4 and SL5. A large array of language features, documented extensively elsewhere [28] [29], make Icon very attractive for a variety of general-purpose application areas, notably text processing and rapid prototyping. Some of these features are

- a familiar syntax reminiscent of Pascal and C,

- generators, goal-directed evaluation, and backtracking,

- a rich set of built-in data structures and operations,

- advanced string scanning and text processing facilities,

- runtime type checking and coercion,

- automatic storage management, and

- invocation mechanisms that include variable number of arguments, and argument defaults for built-in functions.

Icon does not contain the concept of a statement found in most procedural languages. Instead, constructs such as assignments and if-then-else's that are statements in other languages are expressions that can produce values for a surrounding expression in Icon; for this reason, conventional statement-level program monitoring is not well-defined in Icon, and statement-oriented linguistic mechanisms are inadequate in common monitoring situations.

Similarly, the manner in which a program uses Icon's built-in structured data types, scanning facilities, and runtime type coercion has a fundamental effect on program execution behavior [25]. These language features motivate an orientation in execution monitoring that is more directed towards observing the language's built-in, primitive operations and runtime system behavior than would be appropriate for a lower-level conventional procedural language; some of the techniques used for Icon are general, while others are not. For example, while the technique of monitoring program behavior by instrumenting standard library calls is applicable to any language, in C or Pascal there is no incentive to monitor activity during an addition operator to see what it does. In Icon, integer overflow during addition can result in the creation of an arbitrary precision value that is allocated from the heap and might go undetected by a programmer reading the source code.

Within the context of the Icon language, this research addresses several problems that are common to any execution monitoring system. The primary tasks of an execution monitor are to collect information about a program's execution and present that information to the user in an understandable way. In addition to the inherent complexity of these tasks, the main problems posed by execution monitoring in very high-level languages are:

**Volume** — The large amount of data to be processed by the monitor code entails performance problems both in the gathering of information and in the presentation of that information. Efficient gathering of information involves selecting the relevant information from the huge pool of available program behavior data. Efficient presentation of information includes making effective use of the visual medium to communicate with the user, as well as understanding the user's powers of perception. Even if it is gathered and presented efficiently, the large amount of information inherent in monitoring tends to obscure items of interest.

**Dimensionality** — Program execution, although it can be viewed as a sequence of steps executed by the computer, is more completely characterized as a trajectory of a point moving through $n$-dimensional space [53]. For example, at any given instant during execution, an understanding of program behavior can depend on information about current stack depth, source location, heap activity, input/output, and so forth. Each programming language has its own additional dimensions of observable behavior corresponding to its semantics. In addition to behavior related directly to explicit source program operations, very high-level languages also have significant dimensions of implicit runtime system behavior, such as automatic memory management and type conversions.

**Intrusion** — All monitoring systems alter the execution environment of the program under study; when the act of monitoring a program changes the behavior under observation, it is called *intrusion* [2][34]. Henry defines *control-intrusive* and *data-intrusive* methods of adding instrumentation to a program in order to monitor its execution [34]. Control-intrusive instrumentation takes the form of code (such as a procedure call to a monitor routine) embedded within the program. Data intrusion arises in object-oriented systems in which instrumentation is added by subclassing a class to be instrumented and overriding its access methods with additional code. The subclass calls monitor code in addition to calling the superclass method(s) to perform the normal computation. The term intrusion has also been used to refer to the execution slowdown imposed by monitoring [2]; in realtime and concurrent systems, this can render monitoring useless. Since Icon's application domain does not include realtime or concurrent programs, this form of intrusion is not considered in this work. The effect of monitoring on execution speed is considered only so far as to establish framework viability on real Icon programs.

**Access** — Execution monitors often require extensive access to the variables and structures in the program being monitored. If the monitor and program being monitored are distinct programs, operating system constraints may restrict this access, or create performance problems in this area, or both. From the point of view of the execution monitor author, the access problem may also be reflected by low-level or cumbersome notations used to read or write target program data. A good example of access is the traversal of pointers in data structures: if it requires operating system intervention or a notation other than that used in the target program source code, the monitor has poor access to the target program, and the task of writing monitors is made difficult. Solutions to the access problem, such as adding monitor code directly to the program being monitored, often aggravate the intrusion problem.

These problems are universal in execution monitoring and appear repeatedly in the literature. While no general solution for these problems exists, improved monitoring techniques may lessen their severity or solve them for practical purposes on real programs. Traditionally the implementation of execution monitors has been very difficult because the programmers implementing a new monitor necessarily spent a considerable effort addressing these three problems. The difficulty of implementing monitors in turn limits or effectively prevents efforts to improve monitor technology by experimental means.

## 1.4   Contributions

The goal of this research is to reduce the difficulty of constructing execution monitors by developing a practical framework in which monitor construction is relatively easy. The problems identified in the previous section motivate the chosen solutions. The central tenet advocated in this book is the following:

> Source language support for obtaining and presenting execution information is instrumental in the development of exploratory monitoring capabilities in very high-level languages.

The architecture and framework presented in this book provide source language support for the central act of gathering execution information. It addresses the problems of volume, dimensionality, intrusion, and access in the following ways:

**Volume** — Built-in language features for the central act of gathering execution information provide the performance that is necessary for effective monitors written in the source language, despite the generally slower speed of very high-level languages. Dynamic control over the information flow from the program to the monitor is essential for performance.

**Dimensionality** — Multiple monitors simultaneously observe the same program execution and present views along different dimensions of program behavior. Support is provided for monitor communication and the exploratory construction of monitors that specialize in monitor coordination.

**Intrusion** — Language support for gathering execution information from the runtime system eliminates code intrusion. Provision of separate memory allocation areas for the monitor and target program avoids data intrusion.

**Access** — Source language support allows the execution of the monitor and target program in a shared interpeter and provides full source-level access of the monitor to the target program. The framework uses a synchronous coroutine execution model and a shared address space, offering significant advantages without restricting the kinds of monitors that the system supports.

In addition to these features that address core execution monitoring tasks, the framework provides full separation of the program and the various monitors that observe it. Taking the form of dynamic loading and a virtual monitor interface, this separation provides the ease of use that is necessary in order to provide exploratory programming capabilities. The separation allows multiple monitors to observe a program at the same time, and allows new monitors to augment or enhance the capabilities provided by existing monitors.

The intent of the framework is to provide exploratory programming capabilities not just for expert monitor developers, but also for applications programmers who are trying to understand their programs. Given this framework and appropriate library support procedures, writing an execution monitor is no more difficult than writing other applications that involve communication between programs, and often is simpler than writing such applications.

This research is applicable to other high-level languages. Besides the Icon framework described in this book, the same architecture has been implemented for ANSI C, and is relevant to most imperative, functional, logic, and object oriented languages. The specific techniques presented in this book are geared to a very high-level interpretive language; a good test for whether similar techniques would apply to another language is whether the language provides automatic storage management. If it does, the runtime system probably supports other high-level features and makes up a large portion of both the language implementation and the behavior to be monitored. For traditionally compiled systems programming languages, consult the Alamo C framework for different techniques that implement the same monitor architecture [37][67]. The results presented suggest that language designers should provide integral support for monitoring, rather than adding it on as an afterthought.

## 1.5   Overview of This Book

The next two chapters describe prior work in the areas of execution monitoring and fundamental principles of program visualization. Following that, the primary objectives of the framework are presented in Chapter 4. Chapter 5 and Chapter 6 present the underlying mechanism developed to support Icon execution monitoring, and the monitoring instrumentation.

Chapter 7 through Chapter 11 give examples of fundamental monitoring techniques used by many execution monitors, including data collection, presentation, and user interaction techniques. These examples, while simple, demonstrate that the framework makes it possible to develop useful monitors in an exploratory fashion. Chapter 12 discusses monitor communication and gives an example of a coordinator program that allows independently written monitors to be run simultaneously. Chapter 13 includes timing measures that establish the practicality of the framework's performance. Chapter 14 summarizes the work and discusses future research areas. Appendices include larger source code examples and supplementary reference material.

# 2
# Related Work

This book is related to research in two major domains: program execution monitoring, and program visualization. The research presented here contributes to the first category, but is designed to enable new research in the latter category. Consequently, this chapter presents related work in both areas, with a primary emphasis and organization revolving around the execution monitoring aspects of the respective systems. Like this work, a number of earlier systems contribute to both fields; such systems have been called *graphical debuggers* [14]. Existing systems are characterized in terms of three aspects that contribute to usability:

**Information sources and access methods** used by monitors to observe program behavior.

**Execution models** that describe the relationship between the monitor and the program being monitored, and

**User interaction features** such as the information the monitor provides to the user, how information is presented, and the extent to which the user controls and directs monitor activity.

This chapter presents the primary options and tradeoffs inherent in each of these issues, followed by discussions of the design decisions and characteristics of existing systems.

## 2.1   Information Sources and Access Methods

Several methods are used to obtain information about program behavior during execution. Information sources and access methods determine the quality and quantity of the monitoring that can be performed, and are thus a primary design factor in monitoring systems. The method used to obtain information is limited by and often motivates the execution model adopted by a monitoring system. The most common methods are *runtime instrumentation* [44], *manual instrumentation* [10] [66], *interpreter instrumentation* [7] [14] [47], and *instrumenting compilers* [34]. In addition to various methods of instrumentation, some systems provide additional access to program variables and other execution information. This access, if it is present, often makes it possible to monitor behavior not explicitly addressed by the instrumentation.

Runtime instrumentation refers to the modification of the monitored program code immediately prior to or during execution. Modifications often consist of overwriting an instruction of interest with a jump instruction or operating system trap. In either case, control temporarily transfers to code that sends information to the monitor and/or allows the monitor to query the program for information. The code is typically modified in selective areas of interest, and execution proceeds at full speed in other areas.

Manual instrumentation is the insertion of arbitrary monitoring code by hand into the program being monitored. This method is labor-intensive, and requires an instrumentation effort for each program that must be monitored, and additional effort when an instrumented program is modified.

Interpreter instrumentation is the insertion of monitoring code into the language interpreter instead of the program being monitored. The instrumentation can then provide information about the behavior of any program executed by the interpeter.

Instrumenting compilers include preprocessors and code generators that add instrumentation to the code as they produce output. These systems have the potential of automatically instrumenting any program in the language that the compiler recognizes. The code they produce is usually much larger than the non-instrumented code and is usually intended solely for use within the monitoring system.

## 2.2   Execution Models

Of the many models of the relationship between the monitor and the program being monitored used in existing systems, three are primary: the *one-process model* [10] [45], the *two-process model* [44] [61], and the *thread model* [2]. In the one-process model, the monitor consists of a library of procedures linked to the program being monitored or integrated into the runtime system. This is the simplest, highest performance arrangement, and it has the advantage that the monitor has convenient access to the program being monitored. The one-process model is code-intrusive, and errors in the target program or monitor code can affect each other in critical ways. In addition, the control flow logic within the monitor is somewhat inside out, since the monitor is activated strictly through callbacks.

In the two-process model, the monitor is a separate process from the program being monitored. This reduces or eliminates the problems of code and data intrusion, at the expense of greatly complicating monitor access to the state of the program being monitored. This access problem makes monitor construction more difficult, and frequently entails serious performance problems.

In the thread model, the monitor is a separate thread in a shared address space occupied by the program and possibly other monitors. This provides many of the benefits as well as some of the drawbacks of both the one-process model and the two-process model, including the one-process model's risk that program errors in the target program or monitor may affect each other and compromise the monitoring results. The thread model's potential concurrency provides dramatically improved performance for monitoring on shared memory multiprocessors for those forms of monitoring that do not preclude it, such as profilers.

## 2.3  User Interaction Facilities

A primary distinguishing characteristic in existing systems is whether they present material as text or employ graphics to present information. A second distinguishing characteristic is whether a system updates information continuously during execution or provides information during pauses in execution.

User input facilities also vary in existing systems, from controls that can only start and stop execution, to entire languages that can be used to query about execution information during execution or while the monitored program is stopped.

In addition to its uses in controlling the rate of execution and in query facilities, user input in some systems allows the user to modify the program being monitored. This capability is useful in debugging sessions in which an error may be repaired or an alternative value may be substituted. *Program steering* might also fall into the category of deliberate intrusion, especially if the program was not designed to support steering.

The general term *software visualization* is used to denote any graphic depiction of any software artifact, which might or might not be produced by an execution monitor [65]. The subcategory of software visualization tools that are execution monitors employ *program visualization* techniques to provide information to the user. Program visualization refers to the use of graphics to depict program control and/or data at a particular instant, or to continuously update (*animate*) a graphic display to show dynamic behavior as program execution commences. Examples of such tools are the MemMon system for dynamic storage visualization [30] and the Incense data structure visualization tool [49].

The best known area of program visualization is the field of algorithm animation. Some of the most famous examples are Ronald Baecker's motion picture, *Sorting Out Sorting* [4], Marc Brown's research systems BALSA [10] and ZEUS [9], and John Stasko's Tango [66]. The original motivation for algorithm animation was to explain an algorithm to an audience for educational purposes. Since then, it has been applied to a number of tasks including algorithm research. Within these contexts, existing systems have been successful in producing high-quality animations of specific algorithms.

## 2.4    Runtime Instrumentation Systems

Representative runtime instrumentation systems include standard source-level debuggers as well as more general profiling and monitoring systems that modify the code at runtime.

### 2.4.1    Dbx

Dbx is representative of conventional source-level debuggers, the most common form of execution monitor [44]. Source-level debuggers vary widely in their capabilities, but the features of dbx are illustrative of this class of monitors:

- The basic interface is textual in nature. The user specifies both queries and execution controls in a textual command language.

- Execution proceeds, in the default case, just as if the target program were not under the control of the debugger. Ideally, the debugger does not perturb the execution at all. Compiling with debugging support or turning off compiler optimizations in order to debug often perturbs the execution.

- Source code can be displayed as it is executed, in a single step mode.

- Execution can be directed to proceed until a particular point in the source code is reached. Such a point is called a *breakpoint*.

- Breakpoints can be made conditional, testing a predicate (usually expressed in a subset of the source language) in order to determine whether the debugger should be invoked. Unfortunately, conditional breakpoints are "so slow that using this capability is often not practical" [44].

- Program variables can be displayed along with their values; in the case of structures, elements can be displayed and traversed.

- The procedure call chain can be displayed, including parameters passed at each level.

Dbx provides interactive control over program execution at a desirable level—the source language. However, because of language features such as loops and recursion, execution behavior is not proportional to the size of the program source code. The program execution space defined by hand simulation of a running program is orders of magnitude larger than the program source code space. For this reason, source level techniques do not scale well as program size increases. There is simply too much data to monitor, even for common programs of modest size and execution time.

### 2.4.2   Dalek and Duel

Dalek [51] [52] and Duel [20] are source-level debugging systems that deserves further mention in comparison with this book, since they are highly programmable. Both Dalek and Duel are built on top of the GDB debugger [64]. Dalek offers both a special-purpose C-like programming language with which to specify debugging operations and a coarse-grained dataflow approach for recognizing higher abstractions of execution behavior. This combination of features provides a very powerful mechanism for characterizing program behavior of interest. Duel's extension language is higher level and is inspired by Icon, offering generators and goal-directed evaluation.

The flexibility of these systems is limited primarily by the low performance of the underlying UNIX operating system feature that supports debugging in programs like GDB. The ptrace UNIX system interface requires two context switch operations for every word of data obtained by the monitor from the program being debugged [12]. OS memory mapping facilities might alleviate this problem in future systems.

### 2.4.3   cdb and Deet

cdb [33] and Deet [32] are two more recent  machine-independent source-level debuggers. cdb was built for use with lcc [17], while Deet is a portable graphical debugger that supports both C and Java. The low-level operations of these debuggers are encapsulated by *nubs* that allow the remainder of the debugger to be written at a higher level. cdb is interesting in that it can be loaded into the same process as the program being debugged, allowing it to run on systems where process communication and control may not be available. Deet is written in and extensible in both Tcl and the Korn shell. The very high-level language implementation makes it easily to modify and extend, as is the case for Dalek. Deet uses a two-process model and sockets or pipes for communication, resulting in the standard performance bottleneck in debugger automation.

### 2.4.4    Parasight

The Parasight system [2] [3] uses a shared memory  thread model for execution profiling of parallel programs written in conventional languages, such as C. Parasight is designed for conventional languages and the authors compare it to the Berkeley UNIX profiler, gprof. In Parasight the profiler runs on a separate processor and thus has a minimal impact on the execution speed of the program being observed. The thread model provides monitors with complete access to program state. Parasight's user interface includes a C interpreter. The system provides for insertion of additional monitoring instrumentation at runtime by allowing code patching to be applied at any source line number.

### 2.4.5   FIELD

The FIELD programming environment developed at Brown University includes an in-process monitoring facility in which instrumentation is added by code patching [55] [56]. FIELD provides monitoring in the context of a general message based programming environment in which a central message server forwards messages to multiple tools using a *selective broadcast* model. Monitoring instrumentation is bound to application code at link time. During execution, instrumentation code sends messages to the message server; the message server in turn forwards the messages to those tools  that have specified an interest in that type of message. Tools specify which kinds of messages they are interested in when they start executing; this configuration allows the message server to implement the selective broadcast mechanism.

Reiss notes [56] that this general model has significant advantages in easing the integration of new tools into the environment. In addition to the benefits this provides during tool development, the generality of the model offers the advantage that execution monitoring tools coexist with other programming tools geared towards different parts of the program development cycle, such as compilers and cross-referencing tools. Since the message model is based solely on strings, communication of data structures is problematic and creates performance problems.

The Forest system employs a generalization of FIELD's selective broadcast paradigm [19]. In Forest, the central message server maintains dynamic lists of *policies* regarding which tools should receive various events. Dispatching an event requires evaluation of the policies associated with that event. This adds flexibility but places greater computational requirements on the message server.

### 2.4.6   ATOM and EEL

ATOM [62], built on top of OM [63], is a system that executes instrumentation procedures at the time the code is loaded. Instrumentation procedures traverse code in terms of fundamental machine-level elements such as basic blocks, looking for places to add instrumentation. The resulting instrumentation calls analysis procedures directly, avoiding any communication overhead.

EEL [43] is a similar library descended from QP/QPT [42] that offers a lower-level interface with more precise control than is provided by OM and ATOM. Like OM, instrumentation procedures manipulate code in terms of low-level elements abstracted by C++ classes. Unlike OM, EEL is capable of manipulating fully linked (non-relocatable) executables.

Both ATOM and EEL are arbitrarily general, but require the user to perform a low-level imperative programming task in order to obtain instrumentation services. Perhaps the best part about this class of tools is that the program does not have to be recompiled in order to instrument it. In the case of EEL, it does not even have to be relinked.

## 2.5   Manual Instrumentation Systems

Manual instrumentation is frequently employed in systems for algorithm animation. Although tedious, manual instrumentation is also employed during debugging when other debugging tools are ineffective or unavailable.

### 2.5.1   BALSA

In the BALSA system, an animator (often the program's author) augments a well-understood program by inserting calls to the animation library at significant points in the algorithm to convey key aspects to some audience [8]. This code-intrusive approach is suitable for many applications, but Brown notes that if the desired granularity is very detailed, it may involve line-by-line annotations. The applicability of an algorithm animation system such as BALSA is limited if the system does not provide easy access to program state such as the values of variables.

### 2.5.2   Smalltalk

The Smalltalk-80 environment [21] [40], because of its high language level and virtual machine architecture, contains similarities to the Icon interpreter that allow a useful comparison of monitoring techniques in the two languages.

Smalltalk-80 includes three standard monitoring instruments, from which others can be constructed by the user. *Inspectors* allow the user to view or modify the internal state of an object, *notifiers* inform the user of a runtime error or other serious program malfunction, and *debuggers* allow for controlled execution through a piece of code.

These instruments provide the user with detailed access to the state of an executing program at any particular point where execution is stopped. Custom views of the program's current state can be constructed by inheriting from these classes. They do not obtain or present information from a program as it runs.

London and Duisberg developed a kit for algorithm animation of Smalltalk programs [45]. They emphasize detailed views of smaller program examples, for use in industrial prototyping and simulation.

Although instrumentation is manual, in Smalltalk instrumentation can be added by subclassing existing classes and adding monitoring code to various operations in a location that is textually distinct from the original program code. Monitoring instrumentation can also be added by modifying the implementation of various operations along the inheritance hierarchy used by the objects being monitored.

London and Duisberg's animation kit is quite suitable for the algorithm animations it was designed to support, and more generally for understanding tasks that are concerned solely with correctness and not performance. Although instrumentation need not obfuscate the program source text, the technique is data intrusive, since it significantly modifies program behavior in the memory heap. This reduces the system's usability in performance tuning applications, since understanding memory heap behavior is often crucial to understanding performance.

### 2.5.3  Tango

The Tango algorithm animation system, developed at Brown University, emphasizes support for smooth transitions between states in the visualization in order to improve the quality of the animations and reduce the difficulty with which animations are programmed [66]. Tango introduces a path-transition paradigm based on locations, images, paths, and transitions. In addition to smooth transition support, Tango also employs dynamic loading to simplify animation design and shorten the time required to modify an animation.

Tango's goal of supporting exploratory development of algorithm animations is noteworthy. Like BALSA, it employs manual instrumentation of the algorithms being animated; while it is easy to create many animated views of an algorithm in order to choose one that is useful, visualizing new algorithms and larger programs is a major undertaking requiring an understanding of the algorithm to be animated.

### 2.5.4  BEE++

BEE++ is a C++ based monitoring framework developed at CMU [11]. In BEE++, the target program is instrumented with sensors to denote the occurrence of specific events. Some programs might gain instrumentation for free by writing subclasses of classes that were instrumented by others. The event model uses a symmetric peer-to-peer architecture in which both analysis tools and the target program may generate or consume events. Like many systems, BEE++ uses a multi-process execution model and relies on TCP/IP for event delivery, limiting performance but enabling distributed execution of analysis tools on separate machines from target programs. BEE++ supports development of customized graphical debuggers written as subclasses of analyzer classes that are provided with the system.

### 2.5.5   PV

Of all the related work discussed in this chapter, perhaps the project that is most similar to the Alamo system is IBM's PV system [39]. PV provides visualization tools with events for program behavior at multiple levels of abstraction, including operating system and hardware levels not considered in this book. It runs on several IBM architectures such as the RP3 and the RS/6000. PV is trace driven and runs from either *post mortem* traces or from a separate address space during execution. PV is really a hybrid system, not just a manual instrumentation system; it provides automatic instrumentation of lower-level behavior, but higher-level events are hand-instrumented.

In addition to providing program behavioral information at both low and high levels of abstraction, PV advocates a scalable approach to visualization "in the large" that reveals a well-thought-out perspective. Information is presented in multiple, coordinated views. These views show correlations between different behavior. Navigation is coordinated among views. Coarse-grained visualizations show the big picture to start with, and the user clicks on items of interest in order to obtain more detail. In PV, the ultimate level of detail is given by presenting the raw event log to look at individual events, plus the corresponding source code for each one.

## 2.6   Interpreter Instrumentation

Interpreter instrumentation is common for high-level languages, and it is used occasionally in debuggers for lower-level languages. Instrumented interpreters vary widely in the range of features that are instrumented and the nature of the monitoring facilities they provide.

### 2.6.1   SNOBOL4

The SITBOL implementation of SNOBOL4 was extended to include an *event association* facility [31] by which built-in or user-defined functions were associated with significant program events. The program events available for association consisted of variable references, statement executions, program interruptions, function calls and returns, and runtime errors. The SNOBOL4 event association facility is an early example in which monitoring capabilities were implemented in the source language, yet debugging code could be written separately and compiled in with programs when debugging was needed.

### 2.6.2    PECAN

PECAN is an integrated programming environment for an extended dialect of Pascal [54]. It employs multiple views of the static aspects of the program from a single underlying abstract syntax tree. PECAN also includes execution monitoring facilities and can display the current line being executed highlighted in a view of the program source code. PECAN's data visualization capabilities include graphical views of program data structures at break points. Reiss mentions plans to combine PECAN and BALSA to enable program animations.

### 2.6.3    KAESTLE and FooScape

KAESTLE and FooScape provide a visualization system for the Lisp  environment that includes tools for both data and control visualization and provides both static and dynamic views [7]. Their implementation is based upon the FranzLISP tracing system that provides for calls to a monitoring system upon function entry and exit. This system does not allow monitoring of behavior internal to a function, nor can it visualize implicit behavior such as garbage collection. The homogeneous nature of LISP with its simpler control structures and data types mitigates these limitations.

### 2.6.4    Dewlap

Dewar and Cleary developed a Prolog debugger called Dewlap (debugger  with logical applications) that featured graphical displays of the Prolog execution tree [14]. They note that the simplicity of Prolog execution was obscured in earlier Prolog debuggers that employed textual traces of execution. The debugger is written in Prolog, and includes user-definable views of data. The authors observed that Dewlap is too slow to use as a production tools given the speed of their hardware and the interpretive Prolog implementation they used.

## 2.6.5  SeePS

In SeePS, Masnavi animated the internal workings of a NeWS PostScript interpreter by generating Display PostScript windows that reflect the state of various
internal operations [47]. The size and complexity of the program being animated
(an entire language interpreter with hundreds of built-in primitives) take this
project well beyond the realm of algorithm animation.

SeePS was not designed with construction of new visualizations in mind; it was
designed to animate the workings of the language interpreter itself rather than
the execution of the PostScript program being interpreted. This goal is ambitious
as it stands, and since NeWS has sophisticated event handling and lightweight
processes, it represents a challenge to visualization.

The initial approach in SeePS was similar to the one taken in this book: NeWS
source code was augmented to include interesting events; lightweight processes
written in NeWS could then receive such events and generate visualizations for
them. Masnavi cites the benefits of being able to write the visualizations in a
higher-level language and not have to recompile the interpreter in order to modify
a visualization.

In Masnavi's case, this approach was abandoned because it prevented the use of
future, improved versions of the NeWS interpreter, and because SeePS could not
be distributed in such a form. For these reasons, Masnavi rewrote SeePS entirely
in NeWS. This prevents SeePS from visualizing implicit runtime system events;
further, Masnavi notes that SeePS suffers from efficiency problems.

## 2.6.6  Dynascope

Dynascope is a tool for directing the execution of C language programs using
event streams [61]. Event streams are not at the source level, but rather at the
level of the machine instruction for an hypothetical processor. The Dynascope
processor is not a high-level virtual machine such as those used by Smalltalk,
Prolog, or Icon, but rather, it is a low-level architecture typical of current RISC
chips.

Events are produced during the interpretation of code by a virtual machine. Dynascope supports execution of mixed virtual machine and native code programs
and only the parts of a program under observation must be interpreted. In effect,
the monitoring instrumentation and virtual machine interpreter are linked into the
program as an extensive addition to the runtime library.

Dynascope directors are arbitrary programs written independently from the hypothetical processor interpreter; they run in a separate UNIX process connected
using stream-based interprocess communication. This has the distinct advantage
of allowing various directors to be attached to and detached from the system dy-

namically. On the other hand, it means that access to the full program state of the executing program is limited or non-existent.

## 2.7    Instrumenting Compilers

Another alternative to instrumenting a program by hand or instrumenting an interpreter is to modify the translation process to automatically instrument the generated code to include execution monitor calls.

### 2.7.1    Voyeur

Voyeur is a system for visualizing the execution of parallel programs [60]. It is noteworthy in that its authors designed it explicitly to simplify the task of learning how to build views in the system. Voyeur presumes that each new parallel program may require a new visualization, and therefore the system should be easy enough for programmers to construct new views without the aid of an animator specialist as is generally required in BALSA and ZEUS. In their section on future work, the authors note that Voyeur needs access to the program state, support for multiple views, and easier interface construction.

### 2.7.2    UW Illustrating Compiler

The UW illustrating compiler (UWPI) visualizes the execution of programs for a subset of Pascal [34]. It is intended for an educational audience. It is not intended as a framework for exploratory visualization development, but rather, it provides a few fixed views of execution. View selection is performed automatically by static analysis of the program, rather than being user-driven.

UWPI illustrations are driven by calls that are automatically inserted into the code during compilation. Since insertion is automatic, UWPI contrasts with manually code-intrusive systems such as PECAN and BALSA. On the other hand, since the code after analysis includes calls to the illustration system, UWPI can be said to be implicitly code-intrusive. First of all, a program must be specially processed before it can be viewed. Second, after it has been so treated, the result does not run outside the illustration environment. Third, since illustration is driven by explicit calls in the code, the system cannot illustrate implicit runtime behavior, except that which is ascertained by the static analysis component that inserts the illustrator calls.

### 2.7.3  SMLD

The debugger for standard ML, SMLD, uses extensive, automatic instrumentation of the program during compilation [68]. Compiler optimizations reduce the slowdown and code size blowup due to the instrumentation. The instrumentation supports standard debugging features such as setting breakpoints and inspecting the values of variables, but not altering program execution by modifying variables. An extension of SMLD supports reverse execution by means of checkpointing.

## 2.8  Existing Systems Support for Monitor Development

No existing system provides comprehensive support for exploratory execution monitor programming, but if several existing techniques are combined carefully, a suitable framework emerges. The key is to select information sources and access methods, an execution model, and user interaction features that provide ease of programming with acceptable performance. Icon's execution monitoring framework can be viewed as one such configuration of monitoring characteristics.

An instrumented interpreter such as SeePS, or an instrumenting compiler such as Voyeur is potentially an ideal, fully automated information source. An instrumented interpreter is easier to implement, but more importantly, removes the requirement that a program be recompiled in order for it to be monitored. Instrumentation must be extensive or the monitoring capabilities provided will be limited, but extensive instrumentation poses its own performance and intrusion problems. Programming constructs to minimize the impact of instrumentation are essential in dealing with the volume problem in a general-purpose framework.

A thread execution model such as Parasight's provides crucial access and performance features. Monitors that modify the program being monitored require a synchronous execution model if ease of programming is a concern. Also, support for multiple monitors, such as the selective broadcast model developed in FIELD, allows monitors to specialize on specific aspects of program behavior and makes them easier to write. If multiple monitors are to be easily selected and used, the thread model must also include dynamic loading capabilities.

An ideal set of user-interface facilities would support advanced graphics and interaction capabilities, including animation support such as that provided by Tango. This topic is almost unrelated to execution monitoring, but is very necessary in order to provide exploratory programming of state-of-the-art tools. One observation is that interactive user-input is expensive in a highly animated monitor, and specific support in the framework can mitigate this cost by integrating the user input stream with the stream of information coming from the monitored program.

# 3

# Visualization Principles and Techniques

The previous chapter described many monitoring systems' execution models and methods of extracting behavior information from programs that they monitor. These "hard" tasks are the primary subject of this book, but observing behavior is pointless unless information is presented to the user in a way that meets his or her needs. Visualization is the art of presenting large amounts of information in accessible graphical form. Appropriate graphic representations allow the rapid delivery of vast amounts of information that would overwhelm the user if presented in textual form. This chapter introduces the principles that underline effective visualizations, suggests an array of visualization techniques, and presents an incremental methodology by which such tools may be developed.

It is worth noting that there is more than one kind of visualization. *Scientific visualization* is the graphic rendering of gigantic *n*-dimensional data sets by various means of projection and abstraction. In contrast, *software visualization* is the depiction of software artifacts such as directories, user data, or system log files.

*Program visualization* as described in this book is a subfield of software visualization focused on the dynamic behavior of programs themselves, rather than the data they manipulate. The preceding chapter did not present broad coverage of related work in the general area of software visualization, since it has been described admirably in a recent text [65].

Compared with scientific visualization, program visualization is more abstract, since program behavior above the hardware level does not map easily onto real-world geometries. Program visualization evolved from the hand-written diagrams and notations used by programmers and computer scientists to describe their structures prior to the advent of automated visual tools.

## 3.1   Principles

Before there was visualization, there was graphic design. Visualization emerged as a subdiscipline of graphic design when computer screens began to replace printed paper. Visualization includes graphic design, but has additional constraints imposed by hardware and software capabilities and user requirements.

### 3.1.1   Graphic Design Principles

It is not worth implementing elaborate computer graphics if the graphic design does not convey information clearly. Some principles of graphic design are self-evident, such as abstracting away irrelevant detail; other principles are learned through experience. Some of the best references on graphic design are by Tufte [69] [70] [71] and Bertin [6].

Tufte's observations concerning graphic excellence are summed up by the following:

> Graphical excellence is that which gives to the viewer the greatest number of ideas in the shortest time with the least ink in the smallest space.

To achieve such excellence in designs, Tufte advocates five principles:

- if you do nothing else, at least show the information

- show as much as you can with as little ink as possible

- remove ink that isn't showing useful information

- remove redundant information

- revise and edit

The reader may consult Tufte's work for numerous examples of these principles in practice.

Show the Information

If a graphic fails to deliver the required information, it is worse than no graphic. While this mistake might not sound likely, it is not so uncommon for a visualization to present only part of the required information. Depending on the context this can be misleading, or it can be disastrous. Omitting critical information may be as serious as distorting it, a violation of this principle that takes place in myriad forms [35].

Perhaps the most common cause of lost information is when some other information is mapped onto the same location and obscures an item of interest. The viewer may not even know that something is covered up. The situation is not much better if the information is presented but the user cannot decipher it. Visualizations should be self-explanatory. Axes and units, both for geometry and the temporal interpretation of animations, should be clearly explained. On a print graphic, labels and legends might pose an obstacle themselves, but on a computer display they can be toggled on when needed and disappear just as easily.

### Maximize Information Density

A high information density allows more information in the available space, or a given amount of information in a smaller space. Tufte gives published examples that range over between two and three orders of magnitude from the least dense to the most dense! Many computer visualization tools are produced by computer scientists who are experts in fields such as architecture or parallel algorithms and do not bother to study graphic design before they publish their visualization work; not surprisingly, some of these tools achieve monumentally low information density.

Information density is increased by eliminating empty space by either adding more information or shrinking the display. Only the actual information depicted counts toward high density, not labels, legends, axes, arrows, or notes present. If you shrink your display not to the point of unreadability, but to the minimal size it requires, you will make room to run multiple visualization tools side by size. The architecture described in this book supports a large number of simultaneous visualization tools.

High information density comes at a price. Humans have a minimal resolution of perception. Humans can see individual pixels on modern displays, but to perceive discrete objects animated on a screen, the minimal comfortable size may range from one to four pixels square, depending on the resolution and size of the display. Don't rely too heavily on an individual pixel to make an important point.

Information density should be increased in a way that keeps the graphic organized. A dense, complex graphic may be so cluttered that it is difficult to sort out. It turns out that *organized complexity* allows rapid assimilation and is aesthetic in appearance, while *disorganized complexity* is difficult for humans to handle [58].

### Remove Useless Information

Many or most visualization tasks have more information available than room in which to display it. Even if there is enough room, nonessential information

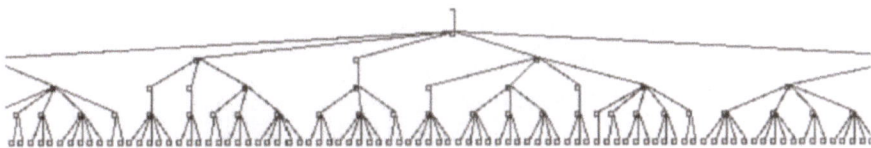

Figure 3.1. A classical tree layout.

distracts and detracts from important information. The user has only so much attention to go around. For this reason, filtering out useless information is a basic task. Of course, not all information can be designated as useless or useful; information occupies a range of utility, especially in visualization situations in which the users are not sure what they are looking for. A corollary of the principle of removing useless information is that the emphasis (and space) allocated to information should be proportional to its usefulness.

Consider drawing common tree structures where many nodes have parent-child relationships, and each node contains its own information. Figure 3.1 shows such a tree using a classically attractive layout algorithm due to Moen [48]. This layout is fine if the user is mainly interested in the size and shape of the tree structure itself; almost all screen space is devoted to structure.

In many applications, however, the user may be more interested in the information presented at the nodes; the tree structure may be a side issue. In this case, a layout such as the tree-map [38] shown in Figure 3.2 may be more relevant, even though its portrayal of the tree structure is less clear. The layout you select for drawing trees should depend on what is important to the user at that particular moment.

### Remove Redundant Information

In user-interface design, it is good for users to have many different ways to accomplish whatever they are trying to do. It is similarly good to have several different ways of viewing data—one way at a time. Providing several simultaneous views of the same data is wasting scarce pixels and resolution that can be better applied to providing a single, richer view. This is even more true for visualization than for ordinary graphics, since visualization typically involves abstracting away a richer set of data than can be portrayed in detail. Useless information is bad, and so is duplicated information.

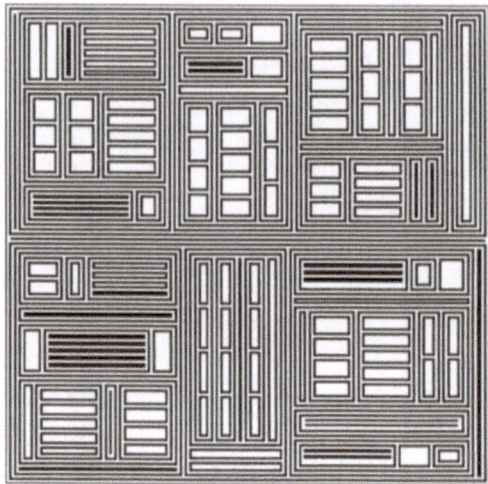

Figure 3.2. A tree-map emphasizes nodes instead of edges.

Iterate

It is naive to expect that your first approach to visualizing something will be optimal. The graphic design will evolve. These refining iterations are costly and time consuming for printed graphics, and they can be equally difficult for visualization programming. Using a language and graphics toolkit that accommodates this principle is common sense.

### 3.1.2   Visualization Principles

Most visualization efforts can start by adapting a well-known technique from printed graphics. Where graphic designers say *ink* one may generally substitute *pixel writes* to the computer's display. A typical bitmapped computer graphics display presents a million or more bytes of information to the user at a time. The raw number of pixels and colors available defines the capability of the display to render static images analogous to print graphics.

Static computer images can be evaluated in terms of graphic design principles such as information density. Most visualizations, however, are dynamic; the graphics hardware and software define limits on the rate at which the display may change. In this context, information density is a three-dimensional measure that includes the time interval during which the changing display is viewed.

Visualization of dynamic execution behavior is different from visualizing a static data set in several ways. These differences motivate the techniques presented in the rest of this book. They may be summarized in the following basic concepts:

- animation
- metaphors
- interconnection
- interaction
- dynamic scale
- static backdrop

Animation

The ability to depict temporal relationships by animating dynamic behavior is a crucial tool. There are tradeoffs between visual sophistication and the associated computational cost and programming time required. Widely applicable techniques are ones that can be animated on low-cost hardware.

Thanks to the computer games market, our definition of low-cost hardware now includes support for animating 3D scenes of moderate complexity. While ubiquitous, many specific workstations and operating systems do not support 3D graphics, so they are not universally available. The hardware is not really the main problem.

The main obstacle to widespread development of animated 3D visualizations is inadequate software. OpenGL, the closest thing to a universal standard, is a low-level specification more oriented towards hardware capabilities than ease of programming. Higher-level languages and toolkits for 3D programming are nonportable, expensive, or both.

In order to achieve universally available, easily programmed animations, this book focuses on simple 2D graphic designs. The output of monitoring could be piped into an existing visualization package such as IDL or Khoros for more sophisticated graphics rendering including 3D views, but this would reduce the degree of interactivity and control provided by the tools.

Least Astonishment

Visualizations should obey the principle of least astonishment. This is important in print graphics, but it is even more important in animated visualizations where the display is changing and the users cannot continuously study each image at their leisure. When possible, visualizations should present information in a manner with which the users are already familiar.

Tufte observes that in the absence of a reason to do otherwise, most graphics should utilize the *golden rectangle*, with a primary horizontal axis 1.6 times wider than the vertical axis. The arguments in favor of the golden rectangle range from human psychology to alleged evolutionary skill at scanning the horizon for predators and prey. Computer displays favor the horizontal axis, albeit with less exaggeration. Text labels are read horizontally and are understood more rapidly when written in a single line than when split onto multiple lines, again favoring a primary horizontal axis. Because most graphics depict information similarly, presentation of data will produce less astonishment when the horizontal axis represents the *cause*, and the vertical axis represents the *effect* described by the graph.

## Visual Metaphors

The mapping from program information to window geometry often is artificial or unintuitive, especially when no natural geometry is inherent in the information to be presented. A familiar or readily inferred visual metaphor for the behavior being presented can lower the cognitive load imposed on the user and increase the rate of comprehension.

Although some metaphors are drawn naturally from a specific application domain or a notation in common use among programmers, others are drawn from nature or from nontechnical symbols found in daily life.

## Interconnection

Understanding a complex piece of software entails an understanding of a variety of distinct behaviors and the relationships between them. For example, control flow, data structures, memory allocation behavior, and input/output all have distinct but interrelated patterns in program execution. Visualizations that consume most or all of the screen do not allow for simultaneous display of other forms of execution behavior.

Under any circumstances, we cannot hope to portray all of program execution in a single 2D or 3D graphic. And we cannot anticipate, in general, which subset of the available information a given user will need. Our emphasis is on multiple visualization tools selected by the user, executing simultaneously, showing different aspects of program behavior.

## Interaction

Visualizations are more effective when the user can navigate and steer them in appropriate directions. Operations such as panning and zooming are vital in order to present some information in more detail than others, because the user remains vital in prioritizing which information to emphasize. The importance of navigation increases in 3D visualizations. Depictions of 3D objects on a computer screen may be ambiguous unless those objects are seen in motion.

A graphic design used in visualization should allow for natural interactive controls, an issue not addressed in static design. For example, a user should be able to select objects and request details about them, or specify that they should be watched, and execution should pause when they are modified.

### Dynamic Scale

The scale imposed in the depiction of dense information on a computer sceen is extreme, but in addition, the scales are highly dynamic. If the scale does not change dynamically, most visualizations waste space and lose detail over most of the execution being observed. On the other hand, changing scale too frequently is both computationally expensive and disorienting.

There are scaling alternatives to redrawing the entire window to use larger or smaller units. There are several different ways to utilize a scale that varies in a single image in a consistent way. If one of these techniques is used, it must be evident to the user or it can work harm instead of help. Logarithmic scales are one option, but they are not always appropriate and typically need to be tuned to the size of the dataset involved.

A more generally useful, but treacherous dynamic scaling technique, is the fisheye view [18]. Fisheye views introduce one or more focus points of attention; a distortion is applied to all output to the window, scaling it by some function of its distance from the focus or foci. Figure 3.3 shows a simple fisheye view with a single focus point applied to a text file. A scalable font and simple arithmetic were all that was needed in order to render this view.

Fisheye views can be applied to arbitrary graphics, and distortion functions may account for multiple focus points with varying degrees of importance [59]. Figure 3.4 shows a map of a simple graph in which each node is distorted by its own factor. The nodes in this case represent solar systems, and they are annotated by orbiting planets and text labels that are all scaled proportional to the size of the star itself, which is drawn as a yellow circle. Planet details and text labels are omitted for systems drawn beneath a minimum threshold size.

### Static Backdrop

Dynamic analysis tools are often best interpreted when superimposed upon a context consisting of information acquired by static analysis; the static information can provide a map that programmers are familiar with. Examples of static backdrops are a program's call graph, or even its source code.

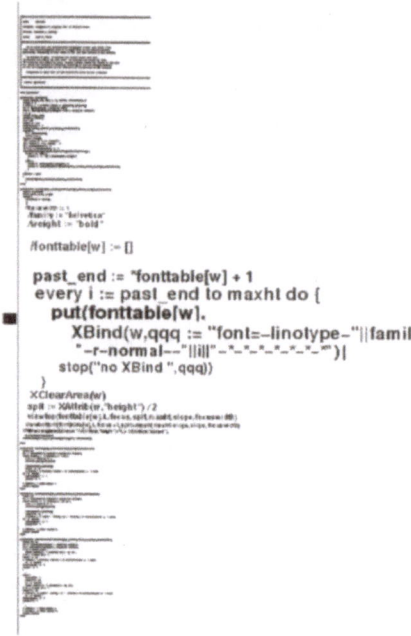

Figure 3.3. A fisheye view with a single focus point.

## 3.2   Techniques

The visualization author faces the problem of rendering the selected graphics with an acceptable real-time performance, characterized by animation frame rate as well as interactive responsiveness and navigability. A visualization can be measured as graphics hardware is measured, in pixels or polygons per second, or the frame rate at which the screen is updated. While this may tell you whether a workstation with faster graphics would improve your visualization, it says nothing about whether the user understood the information. Humans cannot follow details very rapidly, so the optimal rate of change for the graphic display is more likely to be bounded by the human reader than by the hardware or the visualization's graphic rendering algorithm.

Fortunately, some of the simplest graphics are effective, easy to implement, and are familiar to users. Time series graphs, bar charts, pie charts, and scatterplots are all examples of graphic designs that are easily programmed but may need adaptation for visualization purposes. Part III of this book includes many examples of such adaptation.

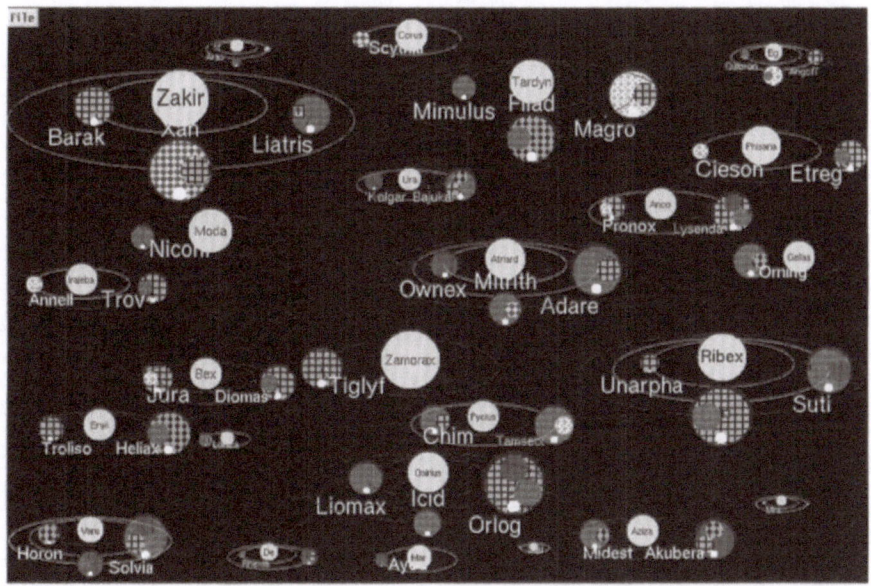

Figure 3.4. A graphical fisheye view (Plate 1).

### 3.2.1  Incremental Algorithms

Redrawing the entire screen each time something changes is not an efficient approach. Incremental algorithms may be required in order to achieve smooth animation. An incremental algorithm is smart enough to render graphics only for the objects on screen that are affected by an operation, and not redraw the others.

It is easy to write incremental algorithms for some graphic designs, and not easy for others. The importance of speedy animation often dictates that a graphic design be selected based on the availability of an incremental algorithm. For this reason, simpler graphic designs may win out over ones that are prettier or more sophisticated.

### 3.2.2  Radial Coordinates

A very interesting visual effect is obtained by adopting a radial mapping in which execution sequence or time rotates around a point. Such mappings are used in a variety of visual metaphors. A radial mapping may represent similar information to that of a Cartesian mapping, but the user may recognize different patterns due

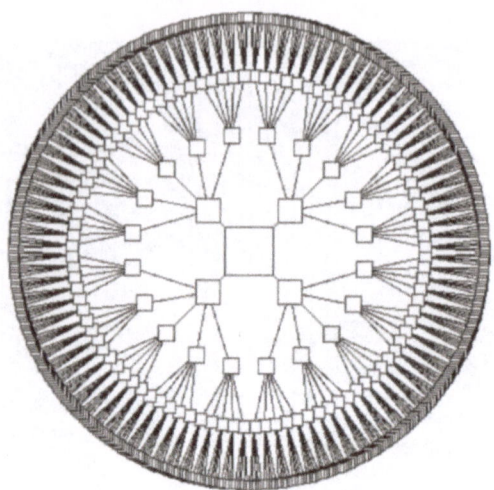

Figure 3.5. A circular tree.

to the metaphor employed. The center of the image provides a natural focus of attention for priority items such as the root of a tree. Figure 3.5 shows a circular tree with hundreds of nodes. More sophisticated radial techniques are possible with the introduction of hyperbolic geometry [41].

If 3D graphics are available, it is possible to obtain the best of both worlds. Radial coordinates may be used to lay out children around their parent at each level, while the third dimension allows the levels of the tree to be separated vertically as in traditional layouts. The result is attractive and scales well to handle large trees. One such layout is the cone tree [57]. Figure 3.6 shows an OpenGL depiction of a cone tree.

Some children may be hidden behind others. As long as the tool provides the ability to rotate subtrees at each node, any node can be brought to the front by some combination of rotations on its ancestors (Figure 3.7).

### 3.2.3   Colors and Textures

Visualizations often have many dimensions of information to depict. Horizontal and vertical coordinates provide two dimensions; animation may grudgingly provide a third. Color and texture provide fourth and fifth dimensions, with limitations.

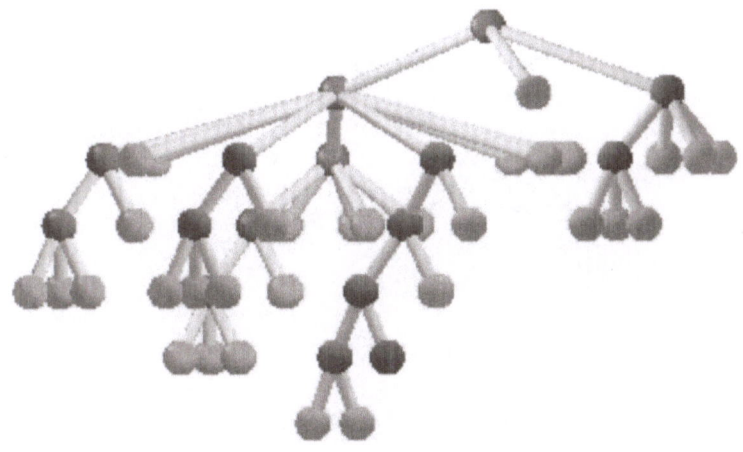

Figure 3.6. A cone tree (Plate 3).

Several basic aspects about colors affect visualization. The number of simultaneous colors on many machines is limited to 256, although hardware standards have been raised to the point that 16- and 24-bit color is common. Visualization techniques are constrained on 256-color hardware. If one visualization tool consumes almost all available colors, other simultaneous visualizations have no colors to choose from. On a 256-color display, the color space can be loosely covered in 216 colors with 6 possible values for each of the red, green, and blue components, and this palette can be shared among visualization tools.

Mapping Numbers to Colors

A ubiquitous temptation in visualization is to use color to represent wide-ranging scalar values such as integers and floats. If you represent an entire numeric value in a single pixel, you have quite a bit better information density than writing out that number textually in a large rectangle of several hundred pixels. This has several limitations and problems, centering on the user's ability to interpret the color encoding correctly.

A 256-color display offers very limited granularity for such color coding. Even on an unlimited display, the human viewer is not likely to associate colors to numbers with a high degree of precision. Regardless of the display used, there is a tendency among untrained programmers writing visualizations to use the color spectrum to depict the range, mapping signed integers onto colors from violet to

Figure 3.7. Rotating subtrees to reveal hidden children (Plate 3).

red. It turns out, though, that humans don't perceive the color spectrum in a linear fashion, so such a mapping is almost useless. Humans can be trained to learn it, but it has no inherent value.

Maps generally use a simpler range of colors to encode elevation using the range of colors one may see on the landscape at varying elevations, ranging from white snowy peaks on mountains to dark blue ocean depths. Such an encoding of numeric values is still quite artificial, but more likely to be usable than a spectrum-based coding. If you use a map-based color coding, at least those people familiar with the encoding will be able to read the numbers in your visualization.

Perhaps the best way of all to map numbers onto colors is to use grayscale. For example, the lowest possible value might correspond to black, while the highest value in the range is depicted as white. Humans are very good at discerning differences in the intensity of colors without changing the hue. For signed numbers, it is quite possible to use separate hues for positive and negative values. A zero value would be represented by a neutral black or white, and large values would progress to vivid red and blue, for example. This approach would be familiar to users of thermometers that depict red as hot and blue as cold.

## Textures and Shapes

Solid area fills are generally better than textured fill patterns, so your first question when contemplating using texture is: can a color or grayscale substitute? Many people are partially or completely colorblind, so textures may be used in place of color to address that problem. The planets depicted in Figure 3.4 show combinations of six different environment types using color and texture simultaneously; the fill patterns are reinforcing the color.

The eternal quest to render multidimensional data leads many programmers to try to depict features using textures and shapes in addition to color. This is usually a mistake, but if you are going to do it, you can at least note some of the following caveats. Any depiction that relies on textures or shapes is trading away resolution for dimensionality, just as dithering trades away resolution to simulate a larger number of colors.

With some exceptions, humans are not very good at memorizing the meanings of textures and shapes. You can get them to admit recognition of 7 +/- 2 textures, such as "vertical stripes" or "crinkled paper," but that's not saying much. Humans can recognize lots more basic shapes such as diamonds or spades, but will still have trouble remembering the corresponding values for a large number of shapes. Also, shapes do not scale down; beneath a certain point they become illegible.

One of the most famous examples of depicting many dimensional data are Chernoff faces, where each multidimensional data point is represented by an entire face with separate values for eyes, ears, nose, and so on. This exploits humans' extensive face recognition training, which starts in early childhood. Humans may be pretty good at telling quickly if two faces are similar, but again each facial component has a small range of effective values; around seven is again a good guess.

# Part II

# An Execution Monitoring Framework for Icon

# 4

# An Overview of the Alamo Architecture

This chapter presents an overview of the Alamo architecture and the execution monitoring framework that has been added to the Icon programming language. Alamo stands for <u>A</u> <u>L</u>ightweight <u>A</u>rchitecture for <u>Mo</u>nitoring, and describes the overall system design. Each implementation of Alamo is a framework for writing execution monitors using some monitoring language to monitor programs in some target language; typically, the monitoring language and target language are the same. So far, Alamo has been implemented for both the Icon and ANSI C languages [37].

The Icon framework described in this book is the more mature of the two frameworks. Since Icon is a very high-level language used for rapid prototyping, the Icon framework is suitable for exploratory development of experimental monitors and visualization tools that can later be implemented for ANSI C using the Alamo C framework.

The Icon framework allows the user to execute a given Icon program under the observation of one or more monitoring programs, also written in Icon. Since the models used and capabilities of execution monitoring systems vary widely, this chapter serves to position the Alamo research with respect to existing systems.

The overview begins with a brief inventory of the Alamo architecture and its components, followed by a user's eye view of a standard Alamo execution monitoring scenario. The purpose of the scenario is to characterize the execution monitoring process that is supported and to motivate some of the features and limitations of the system.

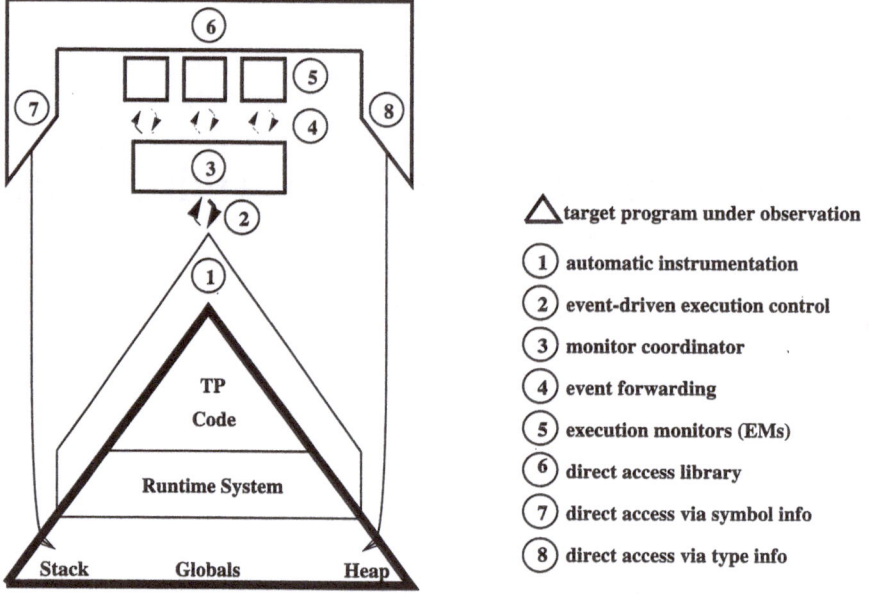

Figure 4.1. The Alamo architecture.

Following the execution monitoring scenario, the functional characteristics of each of the primary components of the execution monitoring framework are described. Details of the use of these components and their implementation are presented in subsequent chapters.

## 4.1   Inventory of Architecture Components

Alamo consists of the following components, summarized in Figure 4.1. Since this book describes the Alamo Icon framework, these components are characterized in terms of their relationship to related Icon features. Several of these components are general-purpose language features that are useful independent of execution monitoring; such features, when already present in other languages, may require modification if they were not designed to support execution monitoring.

**Dynamic loading** — The ability to load multiple programs into a shared execution environment is provided in order to adequately support monitor access to target program data. Prior to this work, Icon had no concept of dynamic loading. *Dynamic linking* is *not* desirable in the context of execution monitoring, since the names in the monitor are distinct from those in the target program.

**Synchronous execution** — The monitor and target program execute independently, but not concurrently. This allows the monitor to control target program execution using a simple programming model. Icon already has a language mechanism and *co-expression* data type that support synchronous execution of independent threads of execution; the mechanism is slightly extended to support the relationship between monitor and target program.

**Automatic high-level instrumentation** — Extensive information about Icon program execution is available to the monitor from locations in the language runtime system that are coded to report significant events. This obviates the need for control-intrusive techniques of obtaining information from the target program. It also offers higher performance than target program instrumentation. The runtime system instrumentation is an extension and generalization of an earlier special-purpose monitoring facility oriented around dynamic memory allocation and reclamation [30]. It also supercedes the language's built-in procedure tracing mechanism [28].

**Event masks** — Monitor control over target program execution is coupled with the concept of *filtering* [16] in a mechanism called an *event mask*. Event masks provide a simple, dynamic model of execution control that adequately meets performance requirements in processing the high volume of execution information. Events that are of no interest to the execution monitor are never reported and do not impose unreasonable execution cost. Event masking uses a set abstraction to describe the execution behavior that is of interest to the monitor; an existing Icon type that supports high performance set operations is employed to provide event masking in a manner that is familiar to Icon programmers.

## 4.2   Standard Execution Monitoring Scenario

Understanding the Alamo architecture begins with a description of the monitoring activities that it supports. The following scenario presents the relationship between execution monitors and target program in its simplest form. More sophisticated relationships between the monitor and target program are discussed later in this chapter and in Chapter 12. In addition, the expected user and range of program behavior observable using Alamo are characterized.

### 4.2.1   Preliminary Definitions

**target program (TP)** — The target program is the Icon program under study, a translated Icon executable file. Monitoring does not require that the TP be recompiled, nor that the TP's Icon source code be available, although some monitors make use of program text to present information.

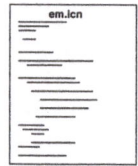

**execution monitor (EM)** — An execution monitor is an Icon program that collects and presents information from an execution of a TP.

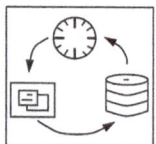

**program behavior** — Program behavior denotes the results of executing the TP. Behavior is meant in a general sense that includes program output, execution time, and the precise sequence of actions that take place during execution.

**user** — In our standard scenario, the user is a human capable of understanding the TP's execution behavior. The user must know the target language in order to make good use of many EMs or to write a new EM. In general, the user need not necessarily be familiar with the TP's source code.

### 4.2.2   Sources of Relevant Execution Behavior

Execution monitoring begins with a user who has questions about the behavior of a TP (Figure 4.2). Typical questions relate to correctness or performance, such as "How is the result calculated?" or "What is taking so long?". Questions may be more general in nature if the user is trying to understand how a program works, rather than to change it.

Answers to important questions often may be found by following the execution as it proceeds through source language constructs, but in high-level languages the behavior in question often depends upon the language semantics as implemented by the language runtime system. In Figure 4.3, iconx.c denotes the aggregate of files that comprise the Icon language runtime system. For this reason, many forms of execution monitoring provide useful information even if the TP's source code is not available. Figure 4.3 could be further elaborated to include behavioral dependencies on the platform on which Icon is implemented and run. Such dependencies are outside the scope of this book.

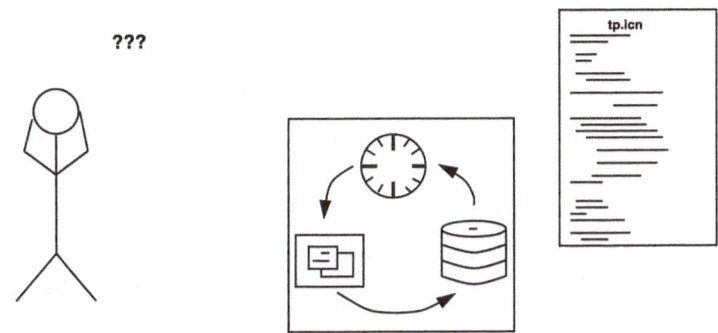

Figure 4.2. Monitoring starts with a user, a program, and questions.

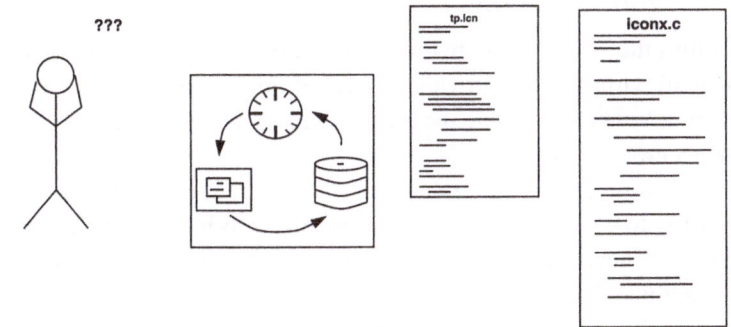

Figure 4.3. Behavior depends on the language, not just the program.

### 4.2.3   Selecting or Developing Appropriate Monitors

Rather than focusing on one monolithic EM that attempts to accommodate all monitoring tasks, the framework advocates development of a suite of specialized EMs that observe and present particular aspects of a TP's behavior. The user is responsible for selecting an appropriate EM or set of EMs that address the user's concerns.

If no available EM can provide the needed information, the user can modify an existing EM or write a new one. This end user development of execution monitors is also useful when an existing EM provides the needed information, but it is obscured by other information; existing EMs can be customized to a particular problem.

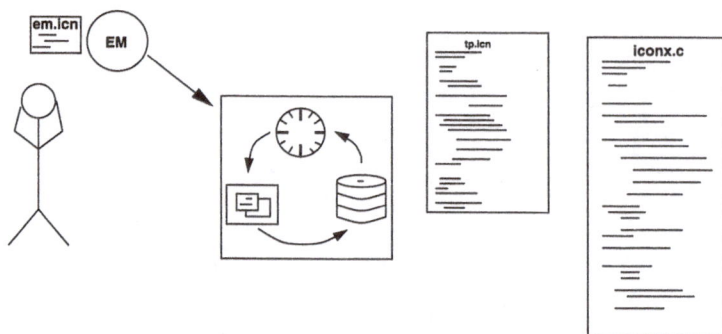

Figure 4.4. EMs can answer questions about TP behavior.

### 4.2.4   Running the Target Program

The user runs the TP one or more times, monitored by a selection of EMs (Figure 4.4). General-purpose EMs provide an overall impression of program behavior. Visualization techniques enable the presentation of a large amount of information and abstract away detail.

Obtaining more specific information frequently requires that the user interact with the EMs to control the TP's execution, either to increase the amount of information presented during specific portions of execution or to stop execution in order to examine details. In order to provide this interactive control, EMs must present execution information as it happens during the TP's execution, rather than during a postmortem analysis phase.

## 4.3   Framework Characteristics

The preceding scenario depends on support for exploratory programming in several areas: controlling a program's execution, obtaining execution information, presenting large quantities of information, and interacting with the user. In order to support these tasks, the framework provides synchronous shared address multitasking and an event-driven execution control model. These features are provided by extensions to the Icon language.

### 4.3.1   Multitasking

The first and most basic characteristic of the framework is an execution model in which an EM is a separate program from the TP—a multitasking model. In this

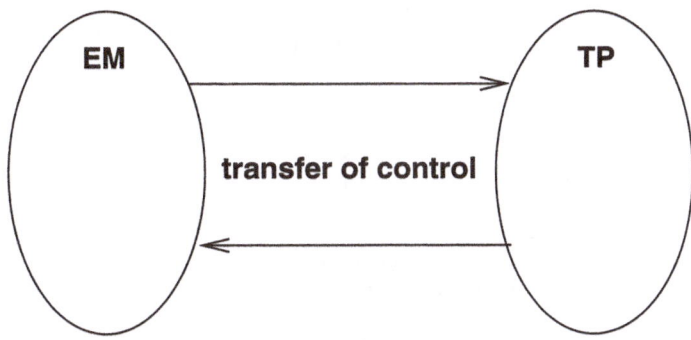

Figure 4.5. EM and TP are separately loaded coroutines.

model the EM views the TP as a separately loaded coroutine [46]. The coroutine relationship is the primary means by which EMs control TP execution, and coroutine transfers of control are the primary source of execution information from a TP (Figure 4.5). The precise nature of the interaction between the EM and TP (the arrows in Figure 4.5) is a major contribution of this research and is discussed further in Section 4.3.2 in this chapter and in Chapter 6.

Multitasking is provided by a set of facilities collectively named MT Icon. MT Icon has the following benefits in an exploratory programming environment: the EM and TP are independent programs, the EM has full access to the TP, and the mechanism accommodates multiple EMs. These benefits are described in more detail below.

Independence

Because the EM and TP are separate programs, the TP need not be modified or even recompiled in order to be monitored by an EM; neither does an EM need modification or recompilation in order to be used on different target programs. The separation of EMs and TPs also simplifies the writing of EMs because an EM need not be implemented as a set of callback functions—it has its own control flow. By definition, execution of tasks such as EMs and TPs is synchronous in MT Icon. The TP is not running when an EM is running, and vice versa. This synchronous execution allows EMs and TPs to be independent without introducing the complexity inherent in concurrent programming.

Another degree of EM and TP independence is afforded by separate memory regions; EMs and TPs allocate memory from separate heaps. For this reason memory allocation in the EM does not affect the allocation and garbage collection patterns in the TP. Because Icon is a type-safe language with runtime type

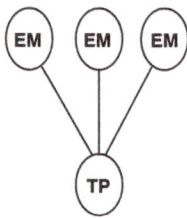

Figure 4.6. Multiple EMs.

checking and no pointer data types, EMs and TPs cannot corrupt each others'
memory by accident; only code that contains explicit references to another program's variables and data can modify that program's behavior. EMs can (and some
do) modify TP values in arbitrary ways; the purpose of separate memory regions
is to minimize *unintentional* data intrusion.

### Access

An address space is a mapping from machine addresses to computer memory.
Within an address space, access to program variables and data is direct, efficient operations such as single machine instructions. Accessing program variables
and data from outside the address space is slower and requires operating system
assistance.

In MT Icon, programs such as the EM and TP reside within the same address
space. This allows EMs to treat TP data values in the same way as their own: EMs
can access TP structures using regular Icon operations, compare TP strings with
their own, and so forth.

Because of the shared address space, the task-switching operation needed to
transfer execution between EMs and TPs is a fast, lightweight operation. This
is important because monitoring requires an extremely large number of task
switches compared to typical multitasking applications.

### Multiple Monitors and Monitor Coordinators

MT Icon's dynamic loading capabilities allow simultaneous execution of not just
a single EM and a single TP, but potentially many EMs, TPs, and other Icon
programs in arbitrary configurations. Although uses for many such configurations
can be found, one configuration merits special attention when many specialized
EMs are available: the execution of multiple monitors on a single TP (Figure 4.6).

The difficulty posed by multiple monitors is not in loading the programs, but
in coordinating and transferring control among several EMs and providing each

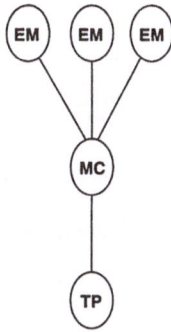

Figure 4.7. An execution monitor coordinator.

EM with the TP execution information it requires. Since EMs are easier to write if they need not be aware of each other, this motivates construction of *monitor coordinators* (MCs), special EMs that monitor a TP and provide monitoring services to one or more additional EMs (Figure 4.7). EMs receiving an MC's services need not be aware of the presence of an MC any more than a TP need be aware of the presence of an EM.

The virtual monitor interface provided by MCs makes adding a new monitor to the system extremely easy. A new monitor could conceivably be written, compiled, linked, and loaded during a pause in the TP's execution. In addition, constructing efficient MCs that provide high- level services is another area of research that is supported within the Alamo Icon framework.

### 4.3.2  Execution Control

The primary task of an EM is to collect data from a TP's execution. This task poses difficult coding problems and is frequently a performance bottleneck. The nature of the data collection facilities available in a monitoring system also define and limit the kinds of monitors that can be implemented.

Figure 4.8 depicts the system layers present in running an Icon program under the Icon interpreter. The TP code is executed by a virtual machine interpreter written in C, which in turn calls C language runtime support code to perform various language operations [27].

Of these layers, the TP code, the virtual machine (VM), and the runtime support code are responsible for aspects of program behavior within the scope of this research. The VM and the runtime system have been extensively instrumented to produce this information for EMs at the Icon level without requiring instrumentation of the TP code.

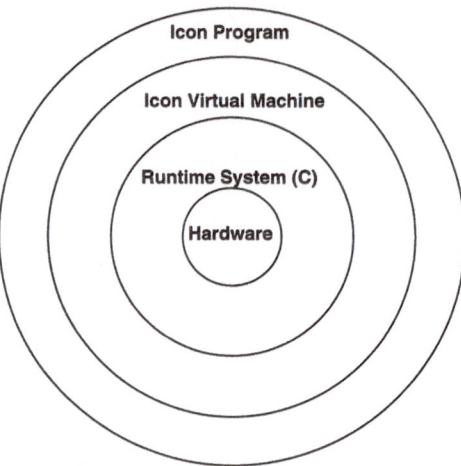

Figure 4.8. Layers in the Icon implementation.

While the behavior observable from instrumentation of the VM is specific to the Icon interpreter and is of interest primarily to language implementors, runtime system behavior is more general and of interest to normal Icon programmers. This book is primarily concerned with monitors of runtime system behavior. Most of this behavior takes place even in compiled versions of the TP, with the exception of behavioral aspects such as runtime type checks that an Icon compiler can avoid when static analysis determines that they are unnecessary.

This instrumentation consists of locations within the runtime system at which control can be transferred and information reported to the EM. When execution proceeds through one of these points in the runtime system, an *event* occurs. Many events take place during even the simplest of Icon operations. When an EM resumes execution of the TP, it explicitly specifies what kinds of events are to be reported; other kinds of events are not reported. The kinds of events to be reported can be changed dynamically each time the TP's execution is resumed (Figure 4.9). The processing of an event includes a test of whether the TP should transfer control to the EM and code to perform the transfer only if the test succeeds.

Those events at which control is transferred produce *event reports*. When an event is reported, the TP's execution is suspended and execution commences in the program that loaded the TP—an EM. Event reporting supports data collection in two ways: an event report contains some information associated with the event itself, and in addition, when the EM gains control, it can interrogate the TP's variables and keywords for further information. When an EM requests another

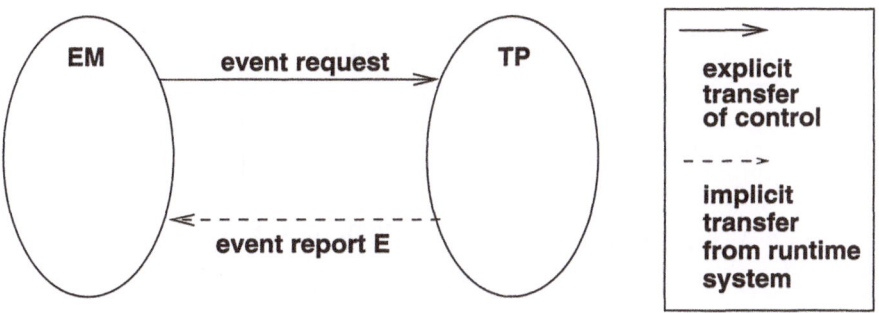

Figure 4.9. Event-driven control of TP.

event report, the EM suspends execution and the TP's execution resumes where it left off.

### 4.3.3  Visualization Support

Alamo explicitly supports graphics output and user interaction in EMs. Given the amount of information associated with the execution of TP, most EMs use graphical techniques to present abstractions of execution information. Since the monitor cannot in general anticipate what information will be relevant or how to interpret it, user interaction is crucial to the success of the monitoring process.

Simplified GUI Programming

Alamo includes a high-level interface to computers' graphical user interface facilities. In the case of Icon, the language provides a built-in window type. The window and any associated window system parameters such as the graphics drawing context and display connection are implicitly bound together as a single Icon value. Programs with a primary window can designate it as the implicit subject of all window operations.

Graphic displays and window system software contain a variety of resources such as colors, fonts, and images. These resources are allocated implicitly by the system when they are used and require minimal attention by the user.

Support for Dual Input Streams

An EM typically has two primary input streams: the event stream from the TP, and the input stream from the user (Figure 4.10). Although these two input streams are conceptually independent and may be treated as such, for many EMs this unnecessarily complicates the central loop that obtains event reports from TP— the EM must also check its own window for user activity.

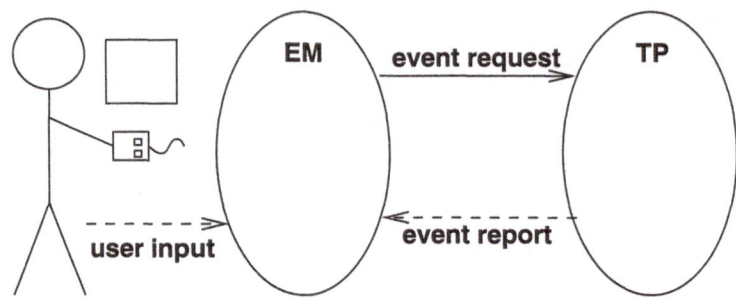

Figure 4.10. Monitors have two input streams.

The runtime system instrumentation includes code that optionally checks for EM input and reports it as an event by the execution monitoring facility, instead of requiring that the EM explicitly check the user input stream. This simplifies EM control flow and improves EM performance.

## 4.4    Comparison with Related Systems

Alamo integrates ideas found in several related systems, allowing useful comparisons. Alamo contributes high-level automatic instrumentation, supplements compile time and runtime filtering methods with dynamic event masking to control the volume of information generated, and unifies the user input and target program event streams present in animated real time visualization tools. The end result is a simplicity in obtaining execution information that achieves the goal of supporting exploratory programming.

Alamo's thread model is synchronous and differs from other thread models that were designed to take advantage of shared memory multiprocessors. Instead, Alamo was designed to simplify the programming task required of monitor writers.

Dalek and DUEL provide programming languages with which to write customized debuggers; their languages are special purpose and must be learned in addition to the user's other responsibilities. In contrast, Alamo monitors are written in a conventional language and compiled with a standard compiler.

Like Alamo, FIELD supports multiple, independent tools that can simultaneously observe program behavior; FIELD is more general since it is a programming environment rather than a monitoring system [56]. Forest extends FIELD's selective broadcast model, adding flexibility comparable to that provided by Alamo [19]. The message server employed by FIELD and Forest is geared toward the use of existing tools such as compilers and editors. This mandates a separate process model and is ill-suited to accommodating the volume of events generated by extensive instrumentation. Alamo does not integrate existing tools, but instead facilitates the development of new experimental monitors.

Alamo simplifies development of execution monitors in several ways, while avoiding common pitfalls associated with monitoring. EMs developed in the Alamo Icon framework tend to be very short compared with those in other systems, because they are developed in a very high-level source language, because they have full access to TP's program variables, and because EMs can specialize on particular program behaviors of interest.

Shorter EMs are in turn easier to understand, to write correctly, and to enhance. Execution monitoring may not be a simple task, but using this system, execution monitors are no more difficult to develop than other programs with substantial interprogram communication requirements. The next two chapters present the Icon language extensions that comprise the execution monitoring framework.

# 5

# A Multitasking Icon Interpreter

This chapter describes MT Icon, a multitasking Icon interpreter that provides key features of Alamo for the Icon language. MT Icon allows multiple Icon programs to be loaded and run simultaneously within a shared address space. Its functionality is general in nature and can be used for purposes other than monitoring. The features of MT Icon are augmented by language facilities that are specific to monitoring; those facilities are described in the next chapter.

## 5.1   Introduction

MT Icon supports multitasking but it is *not* a concurrent programming language nor does it include special support for multiprocessor hardware. Instead, MT Icon provides a task model that supports both cooperative and preemptive multitasking without mandating a particular scheduling policy or algorithm. MT Icon's domain is that of high-level language support for programs that benefit from or require a tighter coupling than that provided by interprocess communication; that is, programs that require extensive access to each other's state.

MT Icon's task model is based on Icon's co-expression facility. This chapter starts with a summary of co-expressions, followed by sections that describe MT Icon language extensions and common applications. In addition to its general multitasking execution model, MT Icon has features specific to the control and monitoring of loaded programs by the program that loads them. The following chapter describes MT Icon's monitoring features in detail.

## 5.2   Co-expressions

A co-expression in Icon is a first class value that encapsulates the execution state of an expression [28]. Co-expressions are the expression level equivalent of the *coroutine* facility found in other languages [46]. A coroutine is a process, specified in terms of a procedure call in which the values of local variables are retained even when control is not within that process, and in which execution upon entry continues from the point where control last left that process. Co-expressions generalize coroutines to allow independent threads of control to be created for arbitrary expressions, not just procedure calls.

   In addition to their role of providing coroutine semantics at a fine granularity of control, co-expressions were developed as a control mechanism necessary to fully utilize the capabilities of Icon's generators [73]. In Icon, a generator is an expression whose evaluation may produce more than one result. This feature is extremely useful and permeates the language, but a generator's results are produced only at the generator's lexical location. Co-expressions liberate generators from their lexical site by placing the expression in a value from which results can be extracted one at a time.

### 5.2.1   Creating Co-expressions

A co-expression value is created by the Icon control structure

> **create** *expr*

When a **create** expression is executed, *expr* is not evaluated; instead, its evaluation is encapsulated as a first class data object that can be assigned to a variable, passed as a parameter, and so forth. In addition to explicitly created co-expressions, a single co-expression is created implicitly when program execution starts; it is equivalent to the expression **create main()**. Program execution begins in this implicit co-expression.

### 5.2.2   Co-expression Transfers of Control

Results are obtained from a co-expression by *activating* it using the operation

> [*expr*] @ *coexpr*

Activation transfers control from the current co-expression to the referenced co-expression; control remains in that co-expression until it produces a result. If the referenced co-expression is subsequently activated, its execution continues from where it last produced a result.

If the *expr* is present in the activation expression, it is evaluated and its result is *transmitted* to the co-expression as control is transferred. If *expr* is omitted, a null value is transmitted.

When each co-expression transfers control only by activating co-expressions it has created or by implicitly producing results for its parent, the control graph formed by co-expressions and their transfers of control is a tree. Explicit transfers of control by co-expression activation may result in an arbitrary control graph, generalizing co-expressions to full coroutine semantics.

### 5.2.3   Co-expression Keywords

In Icon, keywords are named global objects that have special semantics associated with various control structures. Three built-in co-expression values are available to Icon programs in the form of keywords:

> &main  is the co-expression for the invocation of the main procedure that initiates program execution.

> &current  is the co-expression in which execution is currently taking place.

> &source  is the co-expression that activated the currently executing co-expression.

These keywords and their use are further documented in [28].

## 5.3    MT Icon Preliminary Terminology

Before describing the MT Icon task model, a few definitions are needed. These definitions pertain to regions of memory referenced by programs during execution.

### 5.3.1   Name Spaces

A *name space* is a mapping from a set of program source code identifiers to a set of associated memory locations [1]. Icon programs have a global name space shared across the entire program and various name spaces associated with procedures. Procedures each have a static name space consisting of memory locations shared by all invocations of the procedure and local name spaces private to each individual invocation of the procedure.

When a co-expression is created, a new local name space is allocated for the currently executing procedure, and the current values of the local variables are copied into the new name space for subsequent use by the co-expression.

### 5.3.2   Program and Co-expression State

An Icon program has an associated *program state* consisting of the memory associated with global and static name spaces, keywords, and dynamic memory regions. Similarly, a co-expression has an associated *co-expression state* consisting of an evaluation stack that contains the memory used to implement one or more local name spaces. Co-expressions in an Icon program share access to the program state and can use it to communicate.

## 5.4   Tasks: An Extended Co-expression Model

The central concept in MT Icon is the *task*; a task is the execution state of a program within the Icon virtual machine [27]. A single task called the *root* is created when the interpreter starts execution. Additional tasks can be created dynamically as needed.

A task consists of a main co-expression and zero or more child co-expressions that share a program state. At the source language level, tasks are loaded, referenced, and activated solely in terms of one of their member co-expressions; the task itself is implicit.

This definition of tasks is related to the concept of the same name commonly used in operating systems and concurrent programming languages. It differs, however, in certain fundamental respects. Icon is a sequential language; co-expressions in Icon provide a synchronous coroutine execution model, not a concurrent execution model with implicit task switching and scheduling. Another way to view this is that unlike other languages such as Ada, MT Icon provides the task model as a mechanism for multitasking, but does not predefine the policy; matters such as the scheduling algorithm used and whether multitasking is cooperative or preemptive are programmable at the user level.

Another useful comparison can be made between Icon tasks and Smalltalk processes. Both provide pseudo concurrency within the context of a sequential virtual machine. Since Icon tasks have their own dynamic memory regions, their presence affects each other less than Smalltalk processes affect each other. For example, if one task is exhibiting thrashing heap behavior in which garbage collections are frequent, the other tasks in the system can execute at full speed during the portion of time in which they are running, since they do not allocate memory out of the thrashing task's (full) heap. This minimal effect of tasks on each others' behavior is especially important in the domain of execution monitoring.

## 5.4.1    Task Creation

In MT Icon, a task can create other tasks. The MT Icon function

load(s, L, f1, f2, f3, i1, i2, i3)

loads an *icode* file [27] specified by the file name s, creates a task for it, and returns a co-expression corresponding to the invocation of the procedure main(L) in the loaded icode file. L defaults to the empty list. Unlike conventional Icon command-line argument lists, the argument list passed to load() can contain values of any type, such as procedures, lists, and tables in the calling task.

The task being loaded is termed the *child* task, while the task calling load() is termed the *parent*. The collection of all tasks forms a tree of parent-child relationships.

f1, f2, and f3 are files to use as &input, &output, and &error in the loaded task; they default to those of the loading task. i1, i2, and i3 supply initial region sizes in bytes for the task's block, string, and stack memory areas, respectively. The defaults for these sizes may be specified by environment variables BLKSIZE, STRSIZE, and MSTKSIZE.

## 5.4.2    Running Other Programs

A co-expression created by load() is activated like any other co-expression. When activated with the @ operator, the child task begins executing its main procedure. Unless it suspends or activates &source, the child task runs to completion, after which control is returned to the parent. Chapter 6 presents an alternative means of executing a child in which the parent retains control over the child as it executes.

### An Example

This default behavior is illustrated by the program seqload, which loads and executes each of its arguments (string names of executable Icon programs) in turn. In this program the variable arguments is a list of strings passed into the Icon program from the operating system. Each of these strings (extracted from the list using the element generation operator, !) is passed in turn to load(). load() reads the code for each argument and creates a task in which to execute the loaded program; the tasks are then executed one by one by the co-expression activation operator, @. This is ordinary Icon code; there is nothing special about this example except the semantics of the load() function and the independent execution environment (separate global variables, heaps, and so forth) that load() provides to each task.

The child programs can also be used as standalone Icon applications, or can be loaded into other multitasking Icon programs. This approach contrasts with the use of shell scripts or a series of calls to system() to run a sequence of Icon programs.

```
# seqload.icn
procedure main(arguments)
    every @load(!arguments)
end
```

For example, if three Icon programs whose executable files are named translate, assemble, and link are to be run in succession, the command

```
seqload translate assemble link
```

executes the three programs without reloading the interpreter for each program.

## 5.5 Data Access

Although tasks have separate sets of global variables and keywords, they reside in the same address space and can share data. This data access applies to all first-class data objects in Icon, such as procedures and co-expressions. Values can be transmitted from task to task through main()'s argument list, by means of explicit intertask access functions, or by use of event monitoring facilities described in the next chapter.

### 5.5.1  Access Through Task Argument Lists

The following program takes its first argument to be an Icon program to load and execute as a child, sorts its remaining arguments, and supplies them to the child program as its command-line arguments (pop() and sort() are Icon built-in functions that extract the first list element and sort elements, respectively):

```
procedure main(arguments)
    @load(pop(arguments), sort(arguments))
end
```

Argument lists allow more sophisticated data transfers; the seqload example presented earlier can be extended to transmit arbitrary structures between programs using argument lists in the following manner. As in seqload, each string naming an executable Icon program is passed into load(), and the resulting task

is activated to execute the program. In this case, however, any result that is returned by one of the programs is assigned to local variable L and passed to the
next program in the list via the second argument to load().

```
# seqload2.icn
procedure main(arguments)
    every program := !arguments do
        L := @load(program, L)
end
```

The net effect of seqload2.icn is similar to a UNIX pipe, with an important
difference: Arbitrary Icon values can be passed from program to program through
the argument lists. This capability is more interesting in substantial multipass
tools such as compilers, where full data structures can be passed along from tool
to tool instead of writing out text encodings of the structures to a file.

## 5.5.2    Inter-task Access Functions

Several of Icon's built-in functions are enhanced under MT Icon  to provide intertask access to program data. For example, the variable() function in MT Icon
takes a co-expression value as an optional second argument denoting the task
from which to fetch the named variable. When called with this second argument,
variable() is useful for assigning to or simply reading values from another task's
variables. In this modified version of the seqload example, the parent task initializes each child task's Parent global variable (if there is one) to refer to the parent's
&main co-expression. A child task can then use this variable to determine whether
it is being run standalone or under a parent task. Inter-program access through the
variable() function is also useful in inspecting values, especially at intermediate
points during the monitored execution of a TP, as described in the next chapter.

```
# seqload3.icn
procedure main(arguments)
    every arg := !arguments do {
        Task := load(arg)
        variable("Parent", Task) := &main
        @Task
        }
end
```

In addition to MT's extensions of existing functions, several new functions have
been added. These facilities are useful in execution monitoring and are used in
examples in Chapters 7 through 12. Some of the intertask access functions used
in examples are listed in Figure 5.1. In these functions, parameter C refers to a co-
expression that may be from a task other than the one being executed. In proper

| | |
|---|---|
| cofail(C) | transmit failure to C. |
| fieldnames(r) | generate fieldnames of record r. |
| globalnames(C) | generate the names of C's global variables. |
| keyword(s, C) | produces keyword s in C. |
| | Keywords are special global variables that have special semantics in certain language facilities. |
| localnames(C,i) | generates the names of C's local variables, i calls up from the current procedure call. |
| paramnames(C,i) | generates the names of C's parameters. |
| staticnames(C,i) | generates the names of C's static variables. |
| structure(C) | generates the values in C's block region, or heap. The heap holds structure types such as lists and tables. |
| variable(s,C,i) | produces variable named s, interpreted i levels up within C's procedure stack. |

Figure 5.1. MT Icon interprogram access functions.

Icon style, functions that are said to *generate* values can produce more than one result from a given call.

## 5.6  MT Icon Summary

MT Icon provides a general-purpose dynamic loading facility and a synchronous multitasking execution model. It is useful for a variety of applications unrelated to execution monitoring, such as the implementation of shared library facilities, communication of structures between phases of multipass applications, and the development of modular applications in which not all program code need be present at any one time. Because MT Icon's execution model is based directly on Icon's co-expression facility, it encompasses only minimal linguistic changes to Icon. The changes to the implementation were more substantial. More extensive changes to the language, specific to the domain of execution monitoring, are presented in the next chapter.

# 6

# Execution Monitoring in MT Icon

MT Icon allows the execution of multiple Icon programs in almost any configuration, including execution monitoring. As motivated in Chapter 4, MT Icon characterizes monitoring as a special case of multitasking execution in which the nature and extent of interprogram communication warrants additional language support. This chapter describes additional MT Icon facilities specifically added to support monitoring. After some relevant definitions, a description of the programming interface and underlying interpreter instrumentation are given.

## 6.1 Terminology

The terminology used in discussing execution monitoring relates to events and the linguistic features associated with them. These terms are used throughout the rest of the book.

### 6.1.1 Events

The primary linguistic concept added in order to support execution monitoring is an *event*. An event is the smallest unit of execution behavior that is observable by a monitor. In practice, an event is the execution of a point of instrumentation in the code called a *sensor* [50] that is capable of transfering control to the monitor.

This definition limits events to those aspects of program behavior that are instrumented in the language runtime system or the program itself. The event model is only as useful or general as is the instrumentation that extracts program information. If instrumentation does not exist for an aspect of program behavior of interest, it is often possible to monitor the desired behavior by means of other events. In the present implementation, for example, no instrumentation exists for file input and output. If an EM wishes to monitor I/O behavior, it can monitor function and operator events and act on those functions and operators that relate to input and output. A similar example involving the monitoring of Icon's built-in string scanning functions is presented in Chapter 10.

The MT Icon definition of event also differs from that of many monitoring systems, in which the term event refers to the basic unit of information *received* by the monitor [5]. The distinction is that in the MT Icon definition, events occur whether they are monitored or not, and each event may or may not be observed by any particular monitor. This definition is useful in the MT Icon environment, in which EMs are not coupled with the instrumentation and multiple EMs can observe a TP's execution.

## 6.1.2   Event Codes and Values

From the monitor's perspective, an event has two components: an *event code* and an *event value*. The code is generally a one-character string describing what type of event has taken place. For example, the event code C denotes a procedure call event. Event codes all have associated symbolic constants used in program source code. For example the mnemonic for a procedure call event is E_Pcall. These constants are available to programmers as part of a standard event monitoring library described below.

The event value is an Icon value associated with the event. The nature of an event value depends on the corresponding event code. For example, the event value for a procedure call event is an Icon value designating the procedure being called, the event value for a list creation event is the list that was created, the event value for a source location change event is the new source location, and so forth. Event values can be arbitrary Icon structures with pointer semantics; the EM accesses them just like any other source language value.

## 6.1.3   Event Reporting and Masking

The number of events that occurs during a program execution is extremely large—large enough to create serious performance problems in an interactive system. Most EMs function effectively on a small fraction of the available events; the events that an EM uses are said to be *reported* to the EM. An *event report* results in a transfer of control from the TP to the EM. Efficient support for the selection of appropriate events to report and the minimization of the number of event reports are primary concerns.

MT Icon supports *dynamic event masking* based on event codes, a dynamic variation of the filter concept found in most event-based monitoring systems [5] [16]. Event masking allows the monitor to specify which events are to be reported and to change the specification at runtime. When the program being monitored starts execution, the monitor selects a subset of possible event codes from which to receive its first report. The program executes until an event occurs with a selected code, at which time the event is reported. After the monitor has finished processing the report, it transfers control back to the program, again specifying an event mask. Dynamic event masking enables the monitor to change the event mask in between event reports.

The use of one character strings as event codes has a more practical value than its mnemonic merit: it allows sets of codes to be efficiently and easily manipulated at the Icon level by the *cset* (character set) data type. Csets are represented internally by bit vectors, so a cset membership test is very efficient compared to Icon's more generic set data type, whose membership test is a hash table lookup.

When an event report transfers control from TP to EM, the two components of the event are supplied in the Icon keywords &eventcode and &eventvalue, respectively. As discussed in the preceding chapter, these keywords are special global variables that are given their values by the Icon runtime system during an event report, rather than by explicit user assignment. The monitor then can act upon the event based on its code, display or manipulate its value, etc.

## 6.2    Obtaining Events Using evinit

A standard library called evinit provides EMs with a means of obtaining events. Programs wishing to use the standard library include a link declaration such as link evinit. In addition, monitors include a header file named evdefs.icn to obtain the symbolic names of the event codes.

### 6.2.1    Setting Up an Event Stream

An EM first sets up a source of events; the act of monitoring then consists of a loop that requests and processes events from the TP. Execution monitoring is initialized by the procedure EvInit(x[,*input,output,error*]). If x is a string, it is used as an icode file name in a call to the MT Icon function load(). If x is a list, its first argument is taken as the icode file name and the rest of the list is passed in to the loaded function as the arguments to its main procedure. EvInit() assigns the loaded TP's co-expression value to EM's &eventsource keyword. The input, output, and error arguments are files used as the loaded program's standard files.

EMs generally call the library procedure EvTerm() when they complete, passing it their main window (if they use one) as a parameter. EvTerm() informs the user that execution has completed and allows the final screen image to be viewed at the user's leisure, waiting for the user to press a key or mouse button in the window and then closing it.

The typical EM, and all of the EMs presented as examples in this book, follow the general outline:

```
$include "evdefs.icn"
link evinit
procedure main(arguments)
    EvInit(arguments) | stop("can't initialize monitor")
    # ... initialization code, open the EM window
    # ... event processing loop (described below)
    EvTerm()
end
```

This template is generally omitted from program examples for the sake of brevity.

## 6.2.2   EvGet()

Events are requested by an EM using the function EvGet(mask). EvGet(mask) activates the co-expression value of the keyword &eventsource to obtain an event whose code is a member of the cset mask. mask defaults to &cset, the universal set indicating all events are to be reported. The TP executes until an event report takes place; the resulting code and value are assigned to the keywords &eventcode and &eventvalue. EvGet() fails when execution terminates in TP.

### 6.2.3   Event Masks and Value Masks

EvGet() allows a monitor the flexibility to change event masks each time the event source is activated. Another function that sets event masks is eventmask(). eventmask(C,c) sets the event mask of the task owning co-expression C to the cset value given in c.

Event masks are the most basic filtering mechanism in Alamo, but there are situations where they are not specific enough. For example, instead of handling events for all list operations, you may want events only for specific lists. This situation is supported by the concept of *value masks*. A value mask is an Icon set or cset whose members are used to filter events based on their &eventvalue, just as an event mask filters based on the &eventcode. You may specify a different value mask for each event code. Value masks for all event codes are supplied in a single Icon table value whose keys map event codes to corresponding value masks. This table is passed as an optional second parameter to EvGet() or third parameter to eventmask(). Note that no value mask filtering is performed for event codes that are not key in the value mask. Note also that value masks persist across calls to EvGet(). They are replaced when a new value mask is supplied, or disabled if a non-table is passed as the value mask parameter.

There is one special case of value masks that receives extra support in Icon: virtual machine instructions. Requesting an event report for the execution of the next virtual machine instruction is performed by calling EvGet() with an event mask containing E_Opcode. VM instructions occur extremely frequently; dozens of them can occur as a result of the execution of a single line of source code. Consequently, performance is severely affected by the selection of all VM instruction events; the extent of this impact on performance is presented in Chapter 13.

However, a particular instruction or small set of instructions may be of interest to a monitor. In that case, the EM need not receive reports for all instructions. The function opmask(C, c) allows EM to select a subset of virtual machine instructions given by c in C's task. Subsequent calls to EvGet() in which E_Opcode is selected reports events only for the VM instructions designated by c.

The event values for E_Opcode are small non-negative integers. They fall in a limited range ($<$ 256), which is what allows a cset representation for them. Symbolic names for individual virtual machine instructions are defined in the include file opdefs.icn. opmask(C, c) is equivalent to:

```
t := table()
t[E_Opcode] := c
eventmask(C, , t)
```

## 6.3    Instrumentation in the Icon Interpreter

This section describes the instrumentation used by MT Icon to produce events at various points in the runtime system. Significant points in interpreter execution where transfer of control might be warranted are explicitly coded into the runtime system with tests that result in transfer of control to an EM when they succeed. When execution reaches one of these points, an event occurs. Events affect the execution time of the TP; execution is either slowed by a test and branch instruction (if the event is not of interest to the EM), or stopped while the event is reported to the EM and it processes information. Minimizing the slowdown incurred due to the presence of monitoring instrumentation has been a focus of the implementation; inherent costs and framework performance are presented in Chapter 13.

There are several major classes of events that have been instrumented in the MT Icon intepreter. Most of these events correspond to explicit elements within the source code; others designate actions performed implicitly by the runtime system that the programmer may be unaware of. A third class of event that has been instrumented supports user interaction with the EM rather than TP behavior.

## 6.3.1    Explicit Source Related Events

The events that relate behavior observable from the source code are:

**Program location changes** — Source code locations are reported in terms of line numbers and columns.

**Procedure activity** — There are events for procedure calls, returns, failures, suspensions, and resumptions. In addition to these explicit forms of procedure activity, events occur for implicit removals of procedure frames.

**Built-in functions and operations** — Events that correspond to Icon built-ins describe many areas of behavior from numeric and string operations to structure accesses and assignments. Like procedures, events are produced for function and operator calls, returns, suspensions, resumptions, and removals.

**String scanning activity** — Icon's pattern matching operations include scanning environment creation, entry, change in position, and exit. To obtain a complete picture of string scanning, monitors must observe these events along with the built-in functions related to string scanning.

## 6.3.2    Implicit Runtime System Events

Events that depict important program behavior observed within the runtime system include:

**Memory allocations** — Memory is allocated from the string and block regions in the heap. Allocation events include size and type information. This instrumentation is based on earlier instrumentation added to Icon for a memory monitoring and visualization system [30].

**Garbage collections** — The storage region being collected (Icon has separate regions for strings and data structures), the memory layout after compaction, and the completion of garbage collection are reported by several events.

**Type conversions** — In Icon, automatic conversions are performed on parameters to functions and operators. Information is available for conversions attempted, failed, succeeded, and found to be unnecessary.

**Virtual machine instructions** — Icon's semantics may be defined by a sequence of instructions executed by the Icon virtual machine [27]. The program can receive events for all virtual machine instructions, or an arbitrary subset.

**Clock ticks** — The passage of CPU time is indicated by a clock tick.

Most EMs, except completely passive visualizations and profiling tools, provide the user with some degree of control over the monitoring activity and must take user interaction into account. For example, the amount of detail or the rate at which the monitor information is updated may be variables under user control. Since an EM's user input occurs only as often as the user presses keys or moves the mouse, user interaction is typically far less frequent than events in TP. Even if no user input occurs, polling for user input may impose a significant overhead on the EM because it adds code to the central event processing loop.

In order to avoid this overhead, the event monitoring instrumentation includes support for reporting user activity in the EM window as part of the TP's event stream. Monitor interaction events are requested by the event code E_MXevent. An example of the use of monitor interaction events is presented further in this chapter in section 6.5.2, entitled "Handling User Input". A complete list of event codes is presented in Appendix C in order to indicate the extent of the instrumentation.

## 6.4    Artificial Events

As described above, the MT Icon co-expression model allows interprogram communication via explicit co-expression activation or implicit event reporting within the runtime system. *Artificial events* are events produced by explicit Icon code; they can be viewed at the language level as co-expression activations that follow the same protocol as implicit events, assigning to the keyword variables &eventcode and &eventvalue in the co-expression being activated.

There are two general categories of artificial events, *virtual events* meant to be indistinguishable from implicit events and *pseudo events* that convey control messages to an EM. Virtual events are generally used either to produce event reports from manually instrumented locations in the source program, to simulate event reports, or to pass on a real event from the primary EM that received it to one or more secondary EMs. Pseudo events, on the other hand, are used for more general inter-tool communications during the course of monitoring, independent of the TP's execution behavior.

### 6.4.1    Virtual Events Using event()

The function event(code, value, recipient) sends a virtual event report to the co-expression recipient, which defaults to the &main co-expression in the parent of the current task, the same destination to which implicit events are reported.

There are times when a primary EM wants to pass on its events to a secondary EM. An example would be an event transducer that sits in between the EM and TP, and uses its own logic to determine which events are reported to EM with more precision than is provided by the masking mechanism. A transducer might just as easily report extra events with additional information it computes, in addition to those received from TP. A more substantial application of virtual events is a monitor coordinator, an EM that coordinates and produces events for other monitors. Such a tool is presented in Chapter 12.

### 6.4.2  Pseudo Events for Tool Communication

EMs generally have an event processing loop as their central control flow mechanism. The logical way to communicate with such a tool is to send it an event. In order to distinguish a message from a regular event report, the event code must be distinguishable. In the monitoring framework, this is achieved simply by using an event code other than a one-letter string, such as an integer. Since not all EMs handle such events, they are not delivered to an EM unless it passes a non-null second argument (the "value mask argument") to EvGet(), such as EvGet(mask, 1).

The framework defines a minimal set of standard pseudo events, which well-behaved EMs should handle correctly; these pseudo events are described in Chapter 12. Beyond this minimal set, pseudo events allow the execution monitor writer to explore communication between EMs as another facility to ease programming tasks within the monitoring framework.

## 6.5  Monitoring Techniques

The next few chapters demonstrate the potential of MT Icon's execution monitoring facilities with examples of a variety of monitoring techniques. The examples are actual program fragments (rather than pseudocode) that show how to program various forms of monitoring in MT Icon. The purpose of this demonstration is to present MT Icon as a practical language in which to develop exploratory monitors. The examples all follow a common outline and use a common set of facilities, which are described below.

### 6.5.1  Anatomy of an Execution Monitor

The execution monitoring interface presented in this chapter uses a form of *event driven* programming: the central control flow of EM is a loop that executes the TP for some amount of time and then returns control to EM with information in the form of an event report. The central loop of an EM typically looks like:

```
while EvGet(eventmask) do
    case &eventcode of {
        # a case clause for each code in the event mask
        }
```

Event-driven programming is more commonly found in programs that employ a graphical user interface, where user activity dominates control flow. Because monitoring employs a programming paradigm that has been heavily studied, many coding techniques developed for graphical user interface programming, such as the use of callbacks [13], are applicable to monitors. Several of the example EMs in subsequent chapters use a callback model to take advantage of a higher-level monitoring abstraction available by means of a library procedure.

## 6.5.2  *Handling User Input*

An EM that handles user input could do so by polling the window system after each event in the main loop:

```
while EvGet(eventmask) do {
    case &eventcode of {
        # a case clause for each code in the event mask
        }
    # poll the window system for user input
    }
```

If the events being requested from the TP are relatively infrequent, this causes no great problem. However, the more frequent the event reports are, the more overhead is incurred by this approach relative to the execution in TP. In typical EMs, polling for user events may slow execution from an imperceptible amount to as much as 15 percent. Chapter 13 gives the relative frequency of various types of events.

Since the slowdown is a function of the frequency of the event reports and not just the cost of the polling operation itself, techniques such as maintaining a counter and polling once every *n* event reports still impose a significant overhead. In addition, such techniques reduce the responsiveness of the tool to user input and therefore reduce the user's control over execution.

Monitor interaction events, presented earlier in this chapter, address this performance issue by allowing user input to be supplied via the standard event stream produced by EvGet(). Since the E_MXevent event occurs far less frequently than other events, it makes sense to place it last in the case expression that is used to select actions based on the event code. Using this feature, the main loop becomes:

```
while EvGet() do
    case &eventcode of {
        # other cases update image to reflect the event
        E_MXevent: {
            # process user event
            }
        }
```

EvGet() reports pending user activity immediately when it is available; the control over execution it provides is comparable to polling for user input on each event.

### 6.5.3   Querying the Target Program for More Information

After each event report, EMs can use MT Icon's intertask data access functions to query TP for additional information, such as the values of program variables and keywords. The access functions can be used in several ways, such as

- applying a predicate to each event report to make monitoring more specific,

- *sampling* execution behavior not reported by events by polling the TP for information unrelated to the event reports [50], or

- presenting detailed information to the user, such as the contents of variables.

## 6.6   Icon Graphics Capabilities

Icon is best known as a string and list processing language, but it also includes extensive graphics facilities. Visualization tools written in Icon present their output using the type **window**. This section describes only the graphics functions that are used in subsequent chapters. See the book by Griswold, Jeffery, and Townsend for a complete description of Icon's graphics facilities [29].

Windows allow both text and graphic input/output to be freely mixed. While on screen, windows may be moved, resized, and iconified by the user or the Icon program. Window exposure (also known as redraw or paint) events are handled automatically and do not have to be handled by the programmer; the window contents are *retained* until the window closes. If the keyword **&window** has a window value, it serves as a default window for all graphic functions. The remaining examples in this chapter assume **&window** is the window of interest.

Icon's window interface uses a raster graphics model. In this model, a window is a two-dimensional array of points, also called picture elements (*pixels*) in the x- and y-coordinates starting from the pixel (0,0) in the upper-left corner and moving positive to the right and down the window. Several functions take pixel coordinates and draw geometric figures on the window. Pixels are drawn with a window's current *foreground color*.

Some useful functions are given in Figure 6.1; other graphics functions are described as they are used in examples.

Many visualization tools make extensive use of color in graphics operations to encode information about related data types or program operations. Such tools

| EraseArea() | clears a rectangular area |
|---|---|
| DrawArc() | draws an arc |
| DrawPoint() | draws a point |
| DrawLine() | draws a line |
| DrawRectangle() | draws a rectangle |
| DrawString() | draws a string |
| Event() | returns the next user event |
| Fg() | sets the color used in subsequent drawing |
| FillArc() | draws a filled arc |
| FillRectangle() | draws a filled rectangle |
| GotoRC() | moves text cursor position |
| Pending() | returns a list with user events awaiting processing |
| WAttrib(w, attr) | get/set a window attribute such as height or width. |

Figure 6.1. Some useful Icon graphics functions.

could change the output drawing color by repeated calls to Fg(), but it is much faster to ask the window system to set up several window values that draw with different colors. The call Clone(&window, "fg=" || s) creates a window value that draws on &window using foreground color s. All graphics functions may be prefixed with such a window argument w to draw with a nondefault color, for example

```
w_red := Clone(&window, "fg=red")
DrawPoint(w_red, x, y)
```

draws a red point at (x, y).

When an encoding of colors is used in a visualization tool, a table is typically used to store a mapping from a source domain such as string type names to window bindings with various colors.

## 6.7    Some Useful Library Procedures

As mentioned in Section 6.2, several library procedures are useful in EMs. This section presents those library procedures that are included in the evinit library.

Location decoding and encoding procedures are useful in processing location change event values, but they are also useful in other monitors in which two-dimensional screen coordinates must be manipulated. Besides program text line and columns, the technique can variously be applied to individual pixels, to screen line and columns, or to screen grid locations in other application-specific units.

| procedure | returns or computes |
|---|---|
| evnames(s) | converts event codes to text descriptions and vice versa |
| evsyms() | two-way table mapping event codes to their names |
| typebind(w,c) | table mapping codes to color coded Clones for w |
| opnames() | table mapping VM instructions to their names |
| location() | encodes a two dimensional location in an integer |
| vertical() | y/line/row component of a location |
| horizontal() | x/column component of a location |
| prog_len() | number of lines in the source code for TP |
| procedure_name() | name of a procedure |
| WColumns() | window width in text columns |
| WHeight() | window height in pixels |
| WRows() | window height in text rows |
| WWidth() | window width in pixels |

Figure 6.2. Additional library procedures for monitors.

In addition, various EMs use utility procedures. Figure 6.2 lists the library procedures that are used in this book.

## 6.8   Typical Evolution of a Visualization Tool

Many visualization tools can be written by adapting a similar existing tool; in fact, many of the simple visualizations described later in this book are intended as starting points for such programs. Because program visualization is still a relatively undeveloped area, however, there are still frequent situations where a new monitor is written to visualize a new behavior of interest. In such a situation, the monitor writer gets to work from scratch.

While every programmer may approach the task of writing a visualization tool differently, we found over time that a consistent approach has been useful for a wide range of tools. Our method is incremental and reflects the view that the monitoring task is predominant over the graphics programming task in constructing such tools. We present the sequence of tasks here in order to encapsulate this experience. Following the approach is no guarantee that the end product will be successful, but it may simplify for the reader the order in which various components are best assembled.

### 6.8.1    Generate Log Files

The initial emphasis should be to characterize precisely the behavior of interest. Program execution behavior is expressed in terms of a stream of events; events are defined in Chapter 4, and example code for handling them was given earlier in this chapter. A prose description of the behavior of interest may be useful, but a state machine or grammar that describes the event sequences that constitute the behavior of interest is a more useful formalization.

Some behavior will not be described adequately by a regular or context-free sequence of events. In particular, some monitors may have to examine variables and check complex conditions within the program being observed, in order to find the behavior of interest. For these reasons, the ultimate formal preparation prior to writing the visualization code is to produce a fully operational monitor that observes the desired event sequences and writes the relevant events to a logfile. This text-only monitor can be tested to establish confidence in it before starting the task of graphics coding.

### 6.8.2    Depict the Log Files

Once a monitor that observes the correct behavior is written, the primary graphic design and programming can be performed. In the absence of an obvious metaphor, it is possible to start from the same information that was being written to the logfiles and animate it as a sequence of points or more complex objects plotted along a Cartesian or radial axis.

### 6.8.3    Scale to Handle Real Problems

For most monitors, multiple forms of scaling are necessary in order to produce a usable tool from the initial graphic design. Traditional scaling involves multiplying coordinates by a scaling factor in order to ensure that the plotted coordinates do not go outside the visible area of the window. Other forms of scaling begin the conversion from graphs to visualizations. This includes condensation of multiple events down to individual output operations, and of multiple graphic outputs onto a shared space in the window. Several iterations of scaling may be applied as needed.

### 6.8.4    Focus on Behaviors of Interest

Scaling often leads to enough loss of detail that the user cannot see the behaviors of interest, they can only see the big picture. For cataclysmic events of interest, the monitor can help the user notice behaviors of interest by drawing attention to them using flashing lights, sound, or whatever. For more nebulous or tenuous situations, the monitor's goal should be to show enough information for users to decide whether something needs further investigation. Showing more details for atypical behavior is a good starting point. To show more details, the tool requires more screen space. Log scales or hyperbolic or fisheye views allocate conspicuously more screen space to some elements than to others.

### 6.8.5  Add User-Directed Navigation

Ultimately, the user will need to be able to specify objects on the visualization for which additional detailed information is of interest. Adding navigation may be more difficult than rendering the graphics in the first place. The visualization tool will need to perform hit tests to determine which object the user is selecting. This requires a data structure that provides access to on-screen entities, and efficiency may become an issue for very large numbers of objects. This task typically leads to the additional graphics programming required to produce detailed views of objects of interest.

## 6.9  Conclusions

MT Icon includes linguistic facilities to exploit the instrumentation available within Icon's runtime system. By adding language-level support, exploratory development of execution monitors is possible using the Icon lanuage instead of Icon's implementation language, C. Writing a monitor consists of writing an ordinary application in a rapid prototyping language, instead of low-level systems programming that requires intimate knowledge of the Icon implementation. The key concepts introduced for MT Icon's event monitoring facilities are events, event reports, event codes and values, and event masks. Monitors also make use of a standard monitoring library and Icon's graphics facilities.

While the details presented in this chapter are specific to Icon, the results are not. The success of MT Icon's monitoring framework in facilitating construction of new execution monitoring tools is not limited in applicability to Icon—it suggests that if high-quality execution monitors are a priority, designers of high-level languages should consider incorporating monitoring support in the language design rather than leaving it to the ad-hoc devices of some post-implementation afterthought. This support should consist of more than just symbol table information for source variable names.

# Part III

# Writing Visualization Tools

# 7

# Following the Locus of Execution

Perhaps the most basic monitoring act is following along in the source-code as execution progresses. Locus of execution information is used in various tools such as source-code viewers and profilers. Frequently, location information is used in combination with other execution information to inform the user of the specific source code line and column responsible for some behavior of interest.

This chapter presents simple example EMs that monitor location information and present it graphically. The first set of tools shows recent line number changes. These tools are primarily useful in detecting irregular control flow patterns that merit investigation, and in detecting major phases in program execution. Following the line number activity monitors, a graphical location profiler that displays cumulative location information is presented. Profilers are primarily useful in performance tuning.

The examples in this and the next several chapters are intended to demonstrate the broad capabilities of the monitoring framework. Actual source code is given in order to demonstrate useful techniques and affirm the claim that the framework supports an exploratory programming style. While the examples are often suggestive of monitors that are useful in their own right, they are necessarily kept simple for exposition. The development of more sophisticated monitors is an open-ended research domain for future work that this framework was designed to facilitate.

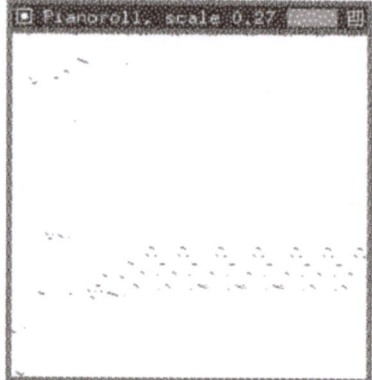

Figure 7.1. A simple line number monitor.

## 7.1    Location Events

An event report with the code E_Loc occurs whenever the source line or column changes. Tracking the execution locus minimally involves selecting this event code in the event mask that is passed to EvGet() along with any others that may be of interest.

The value associated with a change in location is a 32-bit integer encoding of the line and column numbers. The line number is given in the least significant 16 bits, and the column number in the most significant 16 bits.

## 7.2    A Simple Line Number Monitor

The code segment that follows outlines a simple line number monitor that presents the sequence of source code lines on a strip chart. The y coordinate is used to denote the line number; successive line numbers are plotted adjacently along the x axis. Line numbers are scaled to fit the available screen space. A sample screen image is shown in Figure 7.1. The tool is animated, showing the last $n$ line number changes, where $n$ is the width of the monitor window. As the animation progresses, ordinary sequential execution of successive expressions appears in the window as a downward sloping line. Periodic repetitions of patterns in the window indicate the execution of loops.

The EM starts by initializing the event monitoring system and opening a window on which to display its output. Local variables x and y refer to screen coordinates; scale is used to adjust the y coordinate to fit within the bounds of

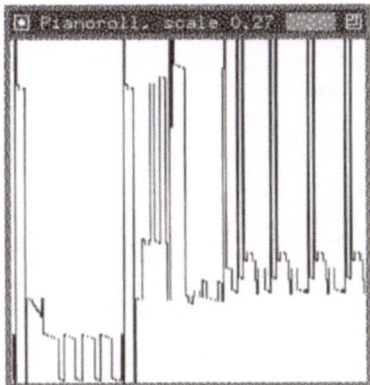

Figure 7.2. Monitoring adjacent pairs of lines.

the window. Real numbers are used in the scaling arithmetic in order to use all of the available window space.

```
&window := open("LineMon", "g", "height=250", "width=250") |
    stop("can't open window")
scale := real(WHeight()) / prog_len()
x := 0
```

The program's main loop reads a location event with a call to EvGet(), computes and scales the line number to the window height, and plots it in the window with a call to DrawPoint(). After the point is plotted, x is advanced to plot the next line number in the next pixel column to the right. When the plot reaches the right edge of the window, the EM wraps around to the left edge. Because pixel columns are reused, a rectangle one pixel wide is erased at each iteration (EraseArea()'s height argument defaults to the entire window).

```
while EvGet(E_Loc) do {
    y := vertical(&eventvalue) * scale
    DrawPoint(x, y)
    x := (x + 1) % WWidth()   # advance x, wrap from right to left
    EraseArea(x, 0, 1)        # clear pixel column for next plot
    }
```

Variations on the line number monitor are presented in Figure 7.2 and Figure 7.3. Figure 7.2 draws a segment between the current source line and the preceding source line at each step. The effect emphasizes large jumps in program location that otherwise might not be noticed due to extremely short visits to certain locations. This phenomenon occurs more frequently in procedures that generate multiple results from a single expression than it does in ordinary proce-

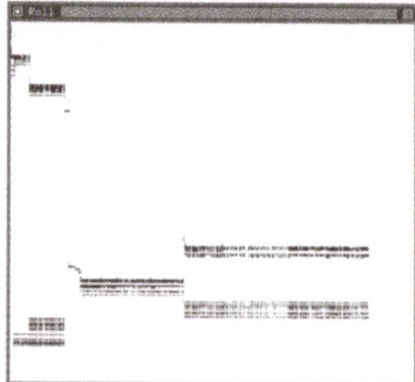

Figure 7.3. Mapping CPU clock ticks to pixel columns.

dural code. Figure 7.3 plots all the lines that execute in a single CPU clock tick (a hardware-dependent value; typically 4-20 milliseconds) in a single column. This view compresses much more location information onto a single screen, but loses the ordering between specific location events within a clock tick.

## 7.3    A Location Profile Scatterplot

Another location monitoring example, presented below, renders a continuously updated scatterplot of program activity by source program line and column number. A sample screen image is presented in Figure 7.4. The tool's animation does not employ motion, but rather changes in color as execution commences. The colors are rendered as grayscales for publication.

This EM maps source code columns and lines onto the x- and y- dimensions, one line or column per pixel. This mapping may be useful or already familiar to the user because it is a miniaturized view of the program text itself. Each source location at which the TP executes is highlighted, with the number of times that location has been executed given by a color progression on a logarithmic scale, from gray and blue through green and yellow and on to orange and red for locations that have executed many times.

The EM starts with standard initialization code and then creates a list of bindings with the various colors. A table, counts, maintains the number of times execution has occurred at each location.

```
&window := open("locus", "g", "bg=white", "size=80,500") |
    stop("can't open window")
Color := [ ]
```

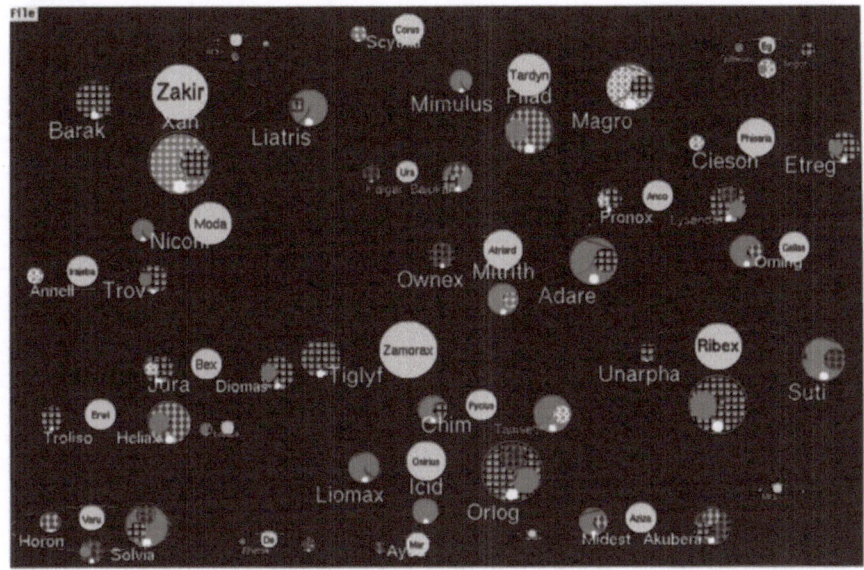

Plate 1. A graphical fisheye view.

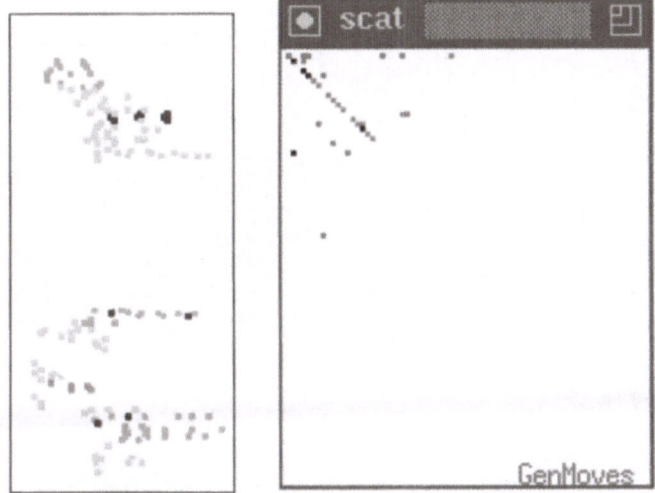

Plate 2. Cumulative (left) and animated (right) profile scatterplots.

Plate 3. Some cone trees.

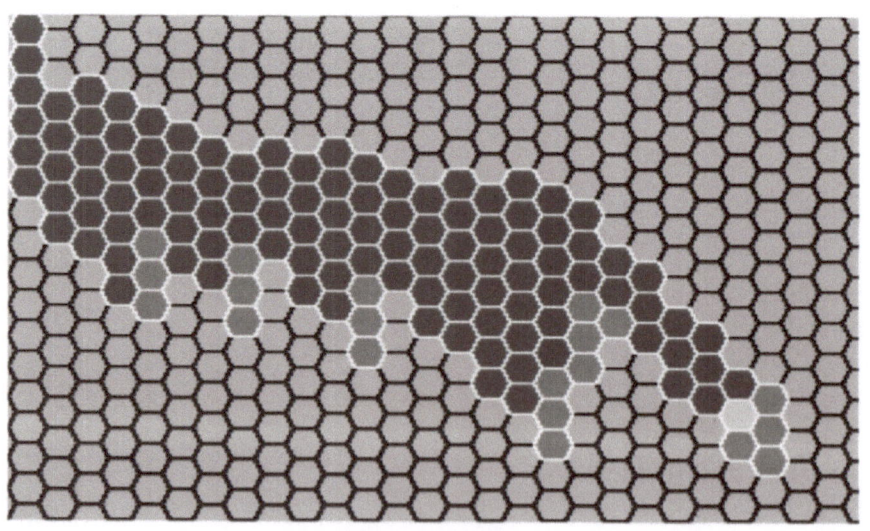

Plate 4. Algae.

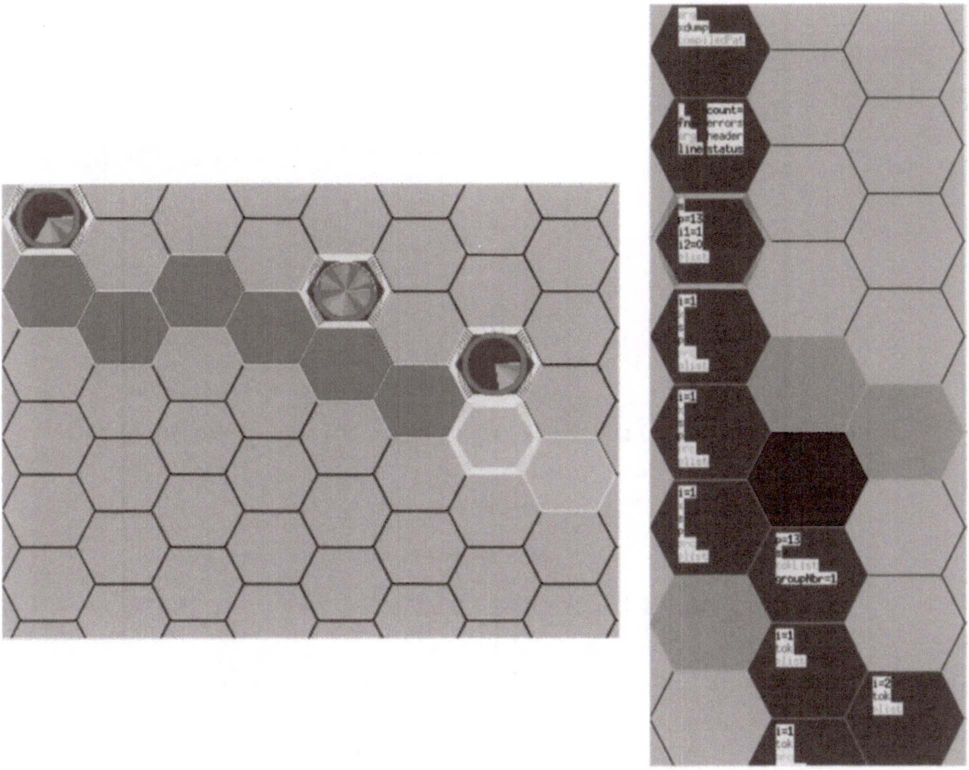

Plate 5. Algae views of string scanning (left) and local variables (right).

Plate 6. Absolute string position.

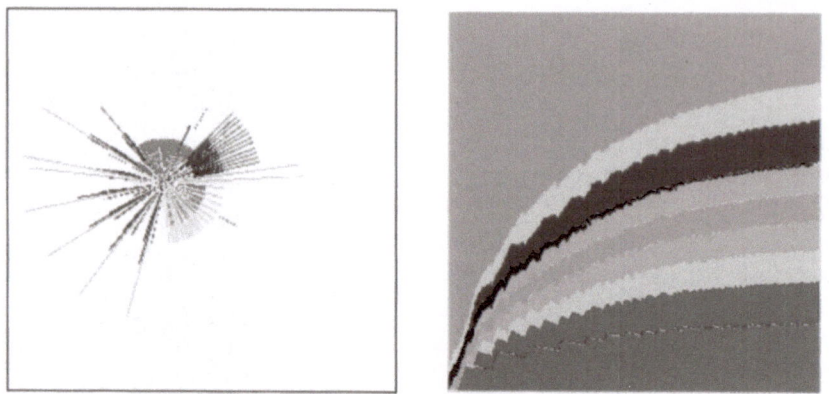

Plate 7. Micro (left) and macro (right) views of memory allocation.

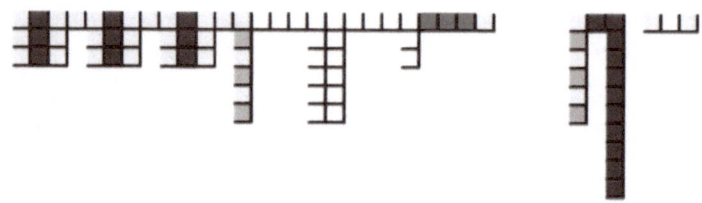

Plate 8. A list access monitor.

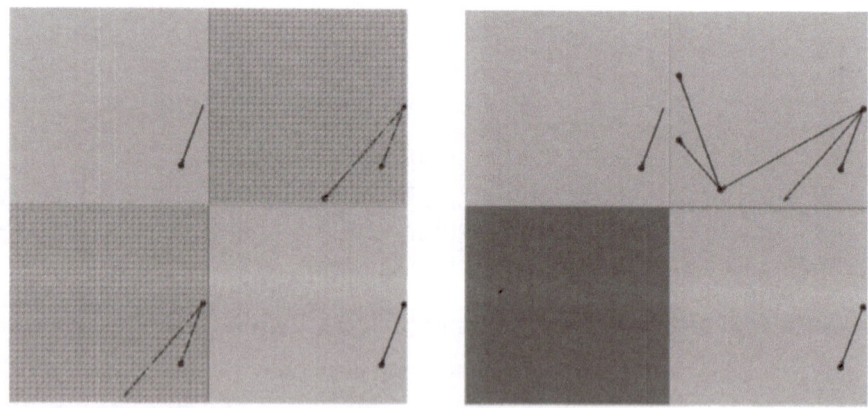

Plate 9. Structure Spy before (left) and after (right) a merge of two components.

Figure 7.4. A location profile scatterplot (Plate 2).

```
every put(Color,
        Clone(&window,
            "fg="||("gray"|"blue"|"green"|"yellow"|"orange"|"red")))
counts := table(0)
```

With initialization completed, the main loop requests a location event, decodes its line and column, and increments the execution count for the location, stored in the table as counts[&eventvalue]. A point is then drawn in the window with a color encoding the log of the location's execution count. If the window height is not large enough to map the source file lines onto pixels, a bar is drawn at the bottom of the window to indicate that it has been clipped. A more sophisticated version of this program scales the mapping from lines to pixels.

```
while EvGet(E_Loc) do {
    y := vertical(&eventvalue)
    x := horizontal(&eventvalue)
    counts[&eventvalue] +:= 1
    value := integer(log(counts[&eventvalue], 6)) + 1
    if Context := Color[ value ] then
        FillRectangle(Context, x − 1, y − 1, 2, 2)
    if y > WHeight() then
        FillRectangle(0, WHeight() − 4, 80, 4)
    }
```

## 7.4   Tracking Source File Changes

Icon programs can be separately compiled. The current source code file at any given point in execution is given by the keyword &file. In a monitoring situation, the current file in the monitored program can be obtained at any instant by querying the value of the &file keyword in the monitored program with the MT Icon function keyword():

source_file := keyword("file", Monitored_Program)

Checking a program's &file keyword is simple and easy, but as the frequency with which the monitor needs this information increases, it becomes equivalent to polling for state information changes. Since minimizing the computational overhead of monitoring can be important, some monitors find it worthwhile to use the event mechanism to reduce the overhead of maintaining source file information.

No explicit event informs programs of source file changes; it must be reconstructed from other events. In the absence of preprocessor directives to the contrary, the source file can only change when execution transfers into a different procedure. In that case, the current source file can be maintained using techniques described in the following chapter on monitoring procedure activity.

# 8

# Monitoring Procedure Activity

Procedure activity is a major aspect of control flow, and it is especially significant in Icon because procedures can generate more than one result. This chapter describes the monitoring of procedure activity in detail. The techniques presented are important because they also apply to the monitoring of Icon's built-in functions and operators as well as string scanning environments. The examples given are intended to illustrate the framework's capabilities and are by no means the best or only way in which procedure activity may be portrayed.

In order to model the semantics of generators, most EMs maintain trees of suspended procedure activations that may be resumed. After presenting techniques to maintain these trees, the chapter describes an EM that draws an animated scatterplot of the number of results that each procedure produces; it quickly shows which procedures are generators, and shows when the number of results a procedure is producing changes significantly. Knowing which procedures are generators can be important for students and program maintainers that are unfamiliar with a program. For programmers that *are* familiar with the target program, knowing the number of results being produced per call to a given procedure can be valuable during debugging; it can confirm expected behavior and/or point out anomalies.

The chapter concludes with an EM that gives an abstract view of the actual tree of active and suspended procedures; it is useful for understanding the path that control flow took to get to the current place of execution. This EM is generalized to include string scanning operations in Chapter 10, and source code for a version

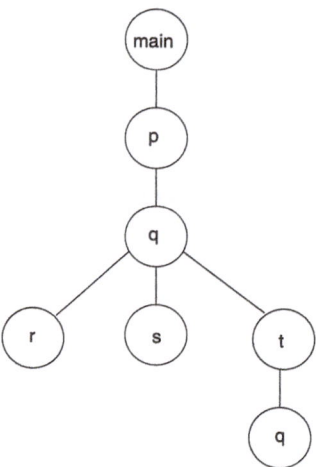

Figure 8.1. An activation tree.

that also allows monitoring of built-in functions and operators is presented in Appendix A as an example of a more sophisticated monitor.

As mentioned in Chapter 6, events take place at procedure calls, suspensions, resumptions, returns, failures, and implicit removals. The constant **ProcMask** contains a cset for all the event codes related to procedures; similar constants **FncMask, OperMask**, and **ScanMask** are used for other types of expression activity.

## 8.1   Activation Trees

The event value for calls and resumptions gives the procedure being activated, but other procedure events such as suspension and return give the Icon value being produced. In order to track the currently active procedure, the monitor must maintain a model of the program's procedure *activation tree* (Figure 8.1).

The procedure **evaltree()** described in this section maintains a simple model of procedure activation trees using records for tree nodes. Each record corresponds to an activation of a procedure. The record contains the procedure, the parent activation record from which the procedure was called, and a list of any children (including suspended ones) that this activation of the procedure has called:

    record activation(value, parent, children)

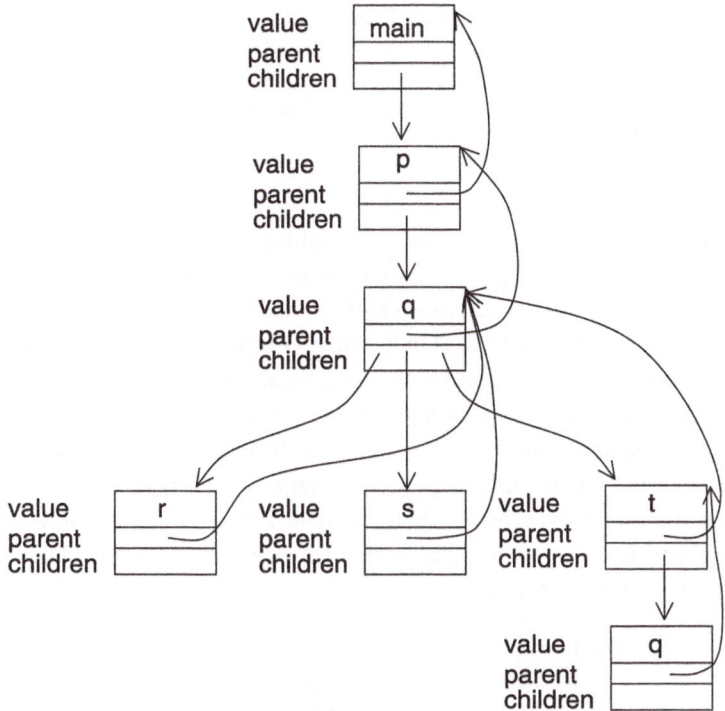

Figure 8.2. An Icon representation of an activation tree.

When used in an EM, the record type may have additional fields to maintain other information about the procedure activation, such as the number of results it has produced. Figure 8.2 shows the Icon structures formed by **evaltree()** to model the activation tree in Figure 8.1. The source code for **evaltree()** is presented in Appendix A.

The procedure **evaltree()** maintains the complete activation tree as well as the current activation with the following monitor event loop. It is called with an event mask parameter and two procedure parameters. The event mask parameter gives all the events needed by the EM. The procedure parameters consist of a call-back procedure used to inform the monitor of changes in the tree, and a record constructor for a record type that has at least the fields declared above. The call-back procedure is called with the activation record being entered as well as the activation record being exited.

```
procedure evaltree(mask, callback, activation_record)
    # compute codes for each branch of the case clause from mask
    while EvGet(mask) do
        case &eventcode of {
            # maintain activation tree, call client callback procedures
        }
end
```

In order to operate properly with any combination of procedure, function, operator, and scanning environment events, evaltree() examines its event mask and builds up lists of codes related to each of the six tree-modifying events. It stores these lists in the global variables CallCodes, SuspendCodes, ResumeCodes, ReturnCodes, FailCodes, and RemoveCodes. In addition, evaltree() creates a dummy root activation on which to build the activation tree.

The branches of evaltree()'s case clause perform the actual tree manipulations and then call the client callback procedure, supplying it with both the activation being entered and the activation being exited. For each call event, a new node is created and inserted as the rightmost child of the current node. The new node becomes the currently executing node.

```
!CallCodes: {
    entered := activation_record()
    entered.node := &eventvalue
    entered.parent := current
    entered.children := []
    put(current.children, entered)
    current := entered
    callback(current, current.parent)
}
```

Return and fail events result in the inverse of a call event: The current node is removed from the activation tree, and the parent of the current node becomes active. When an Icon return expression is executed, the instrumentation produces removal events for all descendants of the returning node preceding the resulting return event.

```
!ReturnCodes | !FailCodes: {
    exited := pull(current.parent.children)
    current := current.parent
    callback(current, exited)
}
```

Suspend and resume events do not change the structure of the tree. For suspend events, the parent becomes the current (active) node; for resume events, the rightmost suspended child is resumed and becomes the current node. After the current node is updated, the client callback procedure is called.

```
!SuspendCodes: {
    current := current.parent
    callback(current, current.children[−1])
    }
!ResumeCodes: {
    current := current.children[−1]
    callback(current, current.parent)
    }
```

Removal events denote the implicit exit of a node in the activation tree as a result of control flow. Typically, a removal event precedes the current node's return or failure and denotes the destruction of the current node's rightmost child. If the current node has no children, removal indicates an implicit destruction of the current node, indicating that it will not be used in the surrounding expression evaluation context.

```
!RemoveCodes: {
    if exited := pull(current.children) then {
        while put(current.children, pop(child.children))
        callback(current, exited)
        }
    else {
        exited := pull(current.parent,children)
        current := current.parent
        callback(current, exited)
        }
    }
```

The default clause in this case expression simply calls the client callback procedure. The activation tree is not modified. This clause is useful because execution monitors that use **evaltree()** may be interested in other types of events besides those that involve the activation tree.

```
default:     callback(current, current)
```

## 8.2   An Animated Call-result Scatterplot

The following example illustrates the use of **evaltree()**, and introduces a simple library for programs that draw animated scatterplots, **scatlib**. This example plots the number of times each procedure has been called along the x axis, while the number of results it has produced is plotted along the y axis. Points are moved

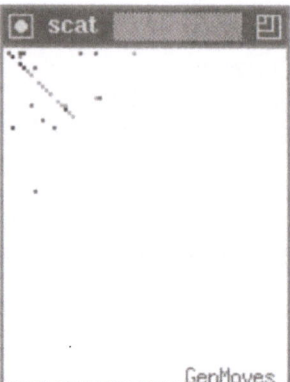

Figure 8.3. A scatterplot with motion (Plate 2).

whenever either a call or a resumption occurs. Red is used for user-defined procedures, while green indicates activity for less expensive built-in functions. If the
user presses a mouse button on one of the plotted points, the names of any procedures plotted at that point are listed. An example screen image from this program
is given in Figure 8.3; the name **GenMoves** in the lower-right corner is the name
of the procedure plotted at the last location on which the mouse was clicked. The
image does not convey the nature of the animation, in which plotted points start
in the upper-left corner and migrate down and to the right at varying speeds and
directions.

A call-result scatterplot serves several purposes. It serves as a basic procedure
call profiler, revealing which procedures are used the most and are therefore most
important in overall performance. Since this information is presented while the
program is executing, it provides quicker feedback than profilers that present
information only after execution has run to completion. Feedback during execution also shows temporal changes associated with major phases in the program.
These uses are language-independent. The call-result scatterplot also serves two
language-specific purposes: it shows the user which procedures are generators,
and how many results the procedures are producing per call.

When a procedure consistently produces no results, it moves horizontally along
the top edge. On the other hand, if a procedure generates results, it moves vertically straight down. If a procedure consistently returns with one result, it moves
diagonally down and across. The slope of a line from the origin to a given procedure's point on this graph gives the average number of results that procedure
has produced per call. If the motion of a point plotted for a procedure changes

its direction substantially, it may indicate unusual behavior that is worth further examination.

### 8.2.1 scatlib

The scatlib library provides animated scatterplot capabilities through a simple interface. The primary function of the library is to track a moving collection of objects that are mapped onto x,y coordinates using a user-supplied scale. Multiple objects may be plotted to the same coordinate. Objects may be plotted using different colors.

### 8.2.2 The Call-result Scatterplot Application

Two global tables, xcounts and ycounts, store the call and result counts for each TP procedure. The global table at maintains a set of objects plotted at each point on the graph; at is keyed by the integer-encoded locations introduced in the preceding chapter and is discussed in more detail later.

```
global    at,          # table of sets of objects at various locations
          xcounts,     # table of x counts
          ycounts      # table of y counts
```

Procedure main() initializes the execution monitoring framework, opens a window, and initializes the scatterplot library by calling scat_init(), and hands off the program's flow of control to evaltree(). evaltree() in turn obtains events, builds the activation tree, and calls scat_callback() for each event report. main() passes scat_callback() to evaltree() as a parameter, in addition to the event mask to use and the record type to use for activations. The event mask includes procedure events selected by the symbol ProcMask and monitor interaction events, indicated by the symbol E_MXevent. Monitor interaction events, described in Chapter 6, provide a convenient means of incorporating user input such as mouse clicks and button presses into EMs without a need for separately polling the EM window for activity.

```
# ... from procedure main()
&window := open("scat","g","width=150","height=180") |
    stop("can't open window")
xcounts := table(0)
ycounts := table(0)
at := table()
evaltree(ProcMask ++ E_MXevent, scat_callback, activation)
```

scat_callback() updates the plotted location of a procedure whenever it is called or produces a result, calling plot() to increase the appropriate procedure's

x- or y-coordinate, respectively. If the event is a call, the point corresponding
to parameter new (the activation being entered) is updated, while if the event is
a suspend or a return, the point corresponding to parameter old (the activation
being exited) is updated.

If the event indicates user activity, a code indicating the user input is supplied
in &eventvalue, and the keywords &x and &y are updated to indicate the mouse
location. If the user presses the escape character "\e", monitoring is terminated;
if the user presses a mouse button, write_names() is called to write the names of
procedures plotted where the mouse indicates.

```
procedure scat_callback(new, old)
    case &eventcode of {
        E_Pcall:              plot(new.node, 1, 0)
        E_Psusp | E_Pret:    plot(old.node, 0, 1)
        E_MXevent: {
            case &eventvalue of {
                "\e": stop("execution halted")
                &lpress: repeat {
                    write_names()
                    if Event() === &lrelease then break
                    }
                }
            }
        }
end
```

The procedure plot() takes a procedure and updates the tables to reflect its new
position. If the procedure is the only occupant of the screen coordinate it is leaving, the point is erased there; similarly, if the new position is not already occupied,
a point is drawn. *Points* are plotted two pixels wide and two pixels high because
individual pixels provide poor visibility on some displays. An even larger size
might improve visibility further at a cost of screen space. plot() uses a logarithmic scale in order to keep the screen size required by this application reasonable
for large programs. A logarithmic scale is chosen over a linear scale because any
linear scale would either plot the most important often-called procedures off the
edge of the chart or else plot all the less frequently called functions together in
one corner of the chart. The scaling process uses the distance of the point from
the origin in order to preserve the ratio of calls to results in the scaled point; this
is discussed in more detail below.

```
procedure plot(who, iscall, isrslt)
    loc := scaled_location(xcounts[who], ycounts[who])
    if *delete(\at[loc], who) = 0 then
        EraseArea(horizontal(loc) * 2, vertical(loc) * 2, 2, 2)
```

```
    xcounts[who] +:= iscall
    ycounts[who] +:= isrslt
    loc := scaled_location(xcounts[who], ycounts[who])
    /at[loc] := set()
    if *insert(at[loc], who) = 1 then
        FillRectangle(horizontal(loc) * 2, vertical(loc) * 2, 2, 2)
end
```

scaled_location(x, y) scales its arguments and produces an integer encoding of the point (x, y) with the x-coordinate in the most significant 16 bits and the y-coordinate in the least significant 16 bits. scaled_location() also computes the distance from the origin for a point using the Pythagorean theorem; it is used during scaling.

```
    procedure scaled_location(x, y)
        length := sqrt(x ^ 2 + y ^ 2)
        return location(scale(y, length), scale(x, length))
    end
```

The procedure scale(coord, len) applies a logarithmic scaling factor to a coordinate. If logarithmic scales were applied separately to the x- and y- coordinates, the proportions of calls to results would not be preserved and the resulting points would be plotted artificially close to the central diagonal of slope 1. Instead, the logarithmic scale is applied to the distance from the origin. The coordinate is multiplied by the ratio of the scaled length to the original length. When both coordinates are so scaled, the scaled point forms a similar triangle to the original unscaled point; the slope of calls to results is preserved from the unscaled point.

```
    procedure scale(coord, length)
        if length < 1 then return 0          # avoid divide by 0 error
        return integer(coord * log(length, 1.25) / length)
    end
```

Procedure write_names() prints the names of all procedures plotted near a mouse click. It builds a list L of the names of all procedures in the at table located within one pixel of the current mouse location. When write_names() has built the list of procedures, it erases the last name list and writes the new list of names in the lower-left corner of the window.

```
    procedure write_names()
        static maxrows, maxcolumns
        &x /:= 2
        &y /:= 2
        # build a list of names of procedures
        L := []
        every i := −1 to 1 do
```

```
every j := −1 to 1 do {
    loc := location(&y + j, &x + i)
    every put(L, procedure_name(!\at[loc]))
    }
# compute the geometry needed to erase last name list
if max := *L[1] then {
    every max <:= *!L
    maxcolumns <:= max
    }
maxrows <:= *L
&col := WColumns() − maxcolumns
&row := WRows() − maxrows − 1
EraseArea(&x, &y)
if *L > 0 then
    every i := 1 to *L do {
        GotoRC(WRows() − *L + i, WColumns() − max)
        writes(&window, L[i])
        }
e := Event()
end
```

The scat program could be generalized in several ways; for instance, it is trivial to extend scat to accommodate Icon's built-in function and operator repertoire. If this information were cross-referenced with static knowledge of which functions and operators were generators, scat could show whether they are being used generatively, or only used to obtain single results as in conventional programming. Another useful way to extend scat would be to allow the user to specify lines (slopes) to indicate a procedure's expected result/call ratio; if the number of results were too low or too high, the user might want to stop execution and inspect the situation in closer detail.

## 8.3   Algae

A program named Algae illustrates one approach to displaying procedure and generation activity in a more connected fashion. Algae displays an animated representation of the activation tree for procedures, built-in functions, and/or string scanning environments as the TP executes, and serves as a basis for other more sophisticated EMs that are presented in later chapters.

Algae is designed to use little screen space and does not require rearrangement of nodes as the tree changes, unlike conventional approaches to tree layout. This attempt to save screen space and animation time produces an approximation of the activation tree that sacrifices the details of parent-child relationships in the

Figure 8.4. Algae (Plate 4).

tree. The Algae metaphor is meant to complement more conventional layouts, not to replace them. The idea behind Algae is to present enough of the expression activity so that common goal-directed evaluation patterns in TP are identified and strange behavior can be noticed as an unfamiliar pattern in the animation.

## 8.3.1  Algae Geometry

The Algae window uses a simple two-dimensional grid of cells; the vertical dimension depicts expression nesting depth, such as calls and returns from procedures. The horizontal dimension depicts generator suspension width, such as procedure, function/operator, and scanning environment suspension. Whenever a computation is suspended, new computations at the same level start in the next cell column to the right, indicating the possibility of backtracking into the suspended computation. A sample image of Algae is shown in Figure 8.4. The target program being monitored is a recursive descent parser. Magenta (depicted as dark gray) cells represent suspended Icon procedures for the nonterminals of a parse that is being attempted. A yellow (light gray) cell in the bottom right is the currently active procedure. Light blue (medium gray) is used to fill in cells when they are vacated; coloring these cells provides a high water mark for the computation up to any given point and gives it an overall characteristic shape.

In order to support the two-dimensional geometry, Algae's activation tree records have fields for the row and the column of the cell assigned for each activation:

record algae_activation(value, parent, children, row, column, color)

Since screen space is limited, each activation is depicted as a small hexagon in the window, color-coded by the kind of activation (procedure, function, operator, or string scanning environment). The size of the hexagons is scalable. Given this geometry, it would be easier to plot Algae using rectangular points. Hexagons are used primarily for their visual effect—they provide a smoother animation as the tree grows and shrinks. Position changes in Algae are often diagonal, and in a square mapping, these changes appear to be a farther distance than horizontal or vertical position changes.

hexlib.icn is a collection of Icon procedures totalling roughly 160 lines that supports the manipulation of hexagon maps; it is omitted here for the sake of brevity. In the code below, the hexlib procedure spot(window, row, column) fills a hexagon at a given location with a particular color.

Because screen space is limited and the activation tree is constantly changing, Algae does not lay out the tree in a way that spreads out nodes throughout the available screen space. Instead, Algae lays out tree nodes from the leftmost edge of the window, being careful to maintain the correct depth and breadth of the tree, and making sure that no two nodes occupy the same cell. When a new node is created, it is a assigned a cell with a row given by its level; the column is computed by inspecting the existing tree and finding the first position to the right of both the parent node and any nodes at the new node's level.

Since expression trees grow and shrink along their rightmost edge, the tree search to assign a column is a preorder, depth-first, right-to-left search. An important special case is if the node's parent already has a child, in which case the newly created node can immediately be assigned a column adjacent to its older sibling; this case is handled directly in algae_callback() for efficiency, and often allows the tree search to be avoided entirely.

The code to compute the column is:

```
procedure computeCol(parent)
    node := parent
    while node.row > 1 do node := \node.parent # find root
    if node === parent then return parent.column
    if col := subcompute(node, parent.row + 1) then
        return max(col, parent.column)
    else
        return parent.column
end
```

```
procedure subcompute(node, row)
    # check this level for correct depth
    if \node.row = row then return node.column + 1
    # search children from right to left
    return subcompute(node.children[*node.children to 1 by −1], row)
end
```

## 8.3.2   *Using* evaltree() *to Incrementally Update the Display*

Algae makes extensive use of colors to indicate the kind of activation, such as whether it is a procedure, function, or string scanning environment. In main(), several bindings are created with different foreground colors, as described in Chapter 6. The colors used are arbitrary and the user can determine the contents of the node by clicking on it if the color is not familiar.

After initialization, Algae calls evaltree() and passes it a reference to the procedure algae_callback(). The event mask used is variable and depends on command-line arguments. The body of algae_callback() performs the incremental animation of the tree. Each event that modifies the activation tree entails the updating of two display cells: a cell that is entered is drawn in yellow to mark it as the active cell, and a cell that is exited is either drawn in the color associated with the activation (if it is suspended) or in a background gray color (if the associated activation has returned or failed and no longer exists).

```
case &eventcode of {
    !CallCodes: {
        new.column := (old.children[−2].column + 1 |
            computeCol(old))
        new.row := old.row + 1
        new.color := Color[&eventcode]
        spot(\old.color, old.row, old.column)
        }
    !RetCodes | !FailCodes:
        spot(background, old.row, old.column)
    !SuspCodes | !ResumCodes:
        spot(old.color, old.row, old.column)
    !RemCodes: {
        spot(black, old.row, old.column)
        WFlush(black)
        delay(100)
        spot(background, old.row, old.column)
        }
    E_MXevent: user_event(&eventvalue, new)
    }
spot(yellow, new.row, new.column)
```

### 8.3.3  Algae Controls

User control of Algae consists of marking specific hexagons (using the left mouse button) or entire rows and columns (using the middle button) to pause execution. Pressing the right button atop a hexagon marked active or suspended prints the name of the associated procedure or function, or the subject of the associated string scanning environment. The input handling is performed by do_event() in response to an E_MXevent.

Each call to algae_callback() checks to see whether the cell being entered is one selected by the user to pause execution, and if it is, the callback procedure loops, reading user events until the user indicates that execution should continue. algae_callback() concludes with thè code for this test:

```
loc := location(new.row, new.column)
if \step | (new.column >= \maxcolumn) |
    (new.row >= \maxrow) | \ hotspots[loc] then {
    step := &null
    WAttrib("windowlabel=Algae stopped: (s)tep (c)ont ( )clear ")
    while e := Event() do
        if user_event(e, new) then break
    WAttrib("windowlabel=Algae")
    }
```

The procedure user_event() returns if execution should proceed, but fails if execution is still paused and another user event should be obtained. The code for user_event() is somewhat lengthy and is included in the complete text of Algae in Appendix A.

## 8.4   Maintaining the Current Source File

The preceding chapter showed a polling technique for obtaining the current source file name in which execution is taking place. Polling is expensive, and for ordinary Icon programs it is better to maintain source file information by tracking the current procedure. The computational load imposed by monitoring can be minimized by only querying &file the first time each procedure is called and maintaining these results in a table. The combined code looks like:

```
source_files := table()
while EvGet(ProcMask) do {
    case &eventcode of {
        E_Pcall: {
            / source_files[&eventvalue] := keyword("file", Monitored)
            current := activation(&eventvalue, current, [ ])
```

```
            put(current.parent.children, current)
            current_file := source_files[current.p]
            }
        E_Psusp: {
            current := current.parent
            current_file := source_files[current.p]
            }
        E_Presum: {
            current := current.children[-1]
            current_file := source_files[current.p]
            }
        E_Pret | E_Pfail: {
            pull(current.parent.children)
            current := current.parent
            current_file := source_files[current.p]
            }
        E_Prem: {
            child := pull(current.children)
            current.children |||:= child.children
            }
        }
    }
```

The techniques presented in this chapter apply not only to procedures, but also Icon's built-in functions, operators, and scanning environments—the evaltree() procedure can accommodate all of these kinds of events simultaneously and maintain one large expression activation tree. Some differences between the different kinds of activations exist; an obvious one is that function and operator events are so frequent that monitoring them in an EM like Algae vastly reduces the tool's effectiveness in monitoring the less frequent procedure activity. It would be useful to explore variants of evaltree() that allow certain subtrees to be ignored, or do not plot activity at all unless interesting behavior such as generation or backtracking takes place.

# 9

# Monitoring Memory Usage

In Icon, memory management is automatic. Memory is allocated when it is needed, and reclaimed implicitly when it is no longer referenced. The memory management subsystem provides significant insight into program behavior. Program performance problems can often be attributed to inefficient memory usage, and the actual pattern of usage can illuminate aspects of behavior ranging from simple transitions between major phases of the program down to semantic errors in program coding.

Memory usage is interesting to study because it is not directly evident from source code examination. The execution monitoring instrumentation produces events on every memory allocation with an event code that indicates the type allocated and a corresponding event value giving the size of the allocation in bytes. In addition, events occur at garbage collections, including the types and sizes of objects that survive reclamation. Allocation events are selected with the evinit symbol AllocMask.

This chapter presents a variety of EMs that portray aspects of memory usage. First, EMs are given that plot each individual allocation in relation to other recent allocations; they are useful in observing localized program behavior such as allocations of unusual size or changes in the major phases of execution. Later in the chapter, EMs that portray cumulative memory usage behavior are discussed; they provide a useful profiling service and a general understanding of the TP's use of memory. These simple examples illustrate only a few of many visual metaphors that have been developed for memory usage, ranging from literal views of the

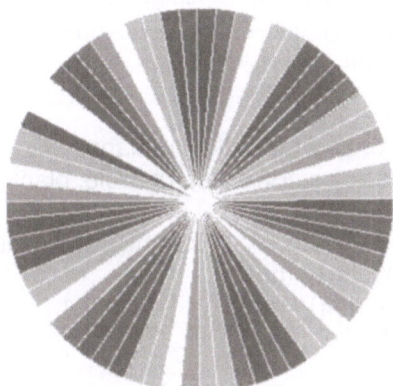

Figure 9.1. Pinwheel.

heap to completely abstract animations whose patterns reflect a program's memory allocations. Some of the other tools that portray memory activity are described in a separate document [26].

## 9.1  Allocation by Type

Many visual metaphors can be used to depict allocation types or sizes, or both. Two allocation monitors are presented in this section. The first emphasizes frequencies and patterns of types in allocated memory, while the second emphasizes allocation size information. These examples also exhibit a clean separation of the data collection and graphics rendering tasks, enabling the visual metaphors to be used in other tools that monitor types of events other than memory allocations.

### 9.1.1  Pinwheel

The pinwheel metaphor presents a sequence of values, in this case the event codes associated with allocation event reports, encoded as colors or textures drawn in sectors around a circle. The $n$ sectors of the circle represent a history of the last $n$ allocation events in the TP's execution. A screen image from a program using this metaphor to present memory allocation patterns is given in Figure 9.1. In this example, event codes for Icon's allocated types are mapped onto colors. The view is updated on each allocation; the animation rate gives an indication of the frequency with which memory allocations occur.

Pinwheel and many other visual metaphors have been encapsulated in procedures for use by execution monitors. By using a common set of conventions, the metaphors can be applied interchangeably and to different types of data. The procedure pinwheel(), called with no arguments, starts with local variable declarations and then initializes several variables that scale the mapping.

```
procedure pinwheel()
    local clear, xorg, yorg, radius, radians
    local angle, arc, sector_units, fullcircle, blank, max, xratio, yratio

    max := real((WWidth() < WHeight()) | WWidth())
    xratio := WWidth() / max
    yratio := WHeight() / max
    fullcircle := 2 * &pi
    radians := 0
    sector_units := fullcircle / Sectors    # amount to advance
    blank := 2 * sector_units               # amount to blank
    xorg := WWidth() / 2
    yorg := WHeight() / 2
    radius := max / 2
    while NextEvent() do {
        FillArc(Background, 0, 0, WWidth(), WHeight(),
            radians + sector_units, blank)
        FillArc(Binding, 0, 0, WWidth(), WHeight(),
            radians, sector_units)
        DrawLine(Background, xorg, yorg,
            xratio * radius * cos(radians) + xorg,
            yratio * radius * sin(radians) + yorg)
        radians +:= advance
        }
end
```

Pinwheel's main loop reads a monitoring event, draws a filled arc in a binding that uses a color associated with the event, and erases the next slice of the pinwheel to mark the edge of motion. The local variable angle, the front edge of the pinwheel motion, is advanced at each iteration. The procedure NextEvent() encapsulates the task of reading a program event and selecting an appropriate color (or texture) to portray it so that the type of data being processed and the color used to draw the pinwheel are independent of the task of drawing the pinwheel itself. NextEvent() assigns the global variable Binding a window value with an appropriate foreground color for use in drawing the sector.

## 9.1.2   Nova

The nova metaphor is another example of a radial mapping of a sequence of event reports. Each allocation event report is plotted as a line segment from the center of

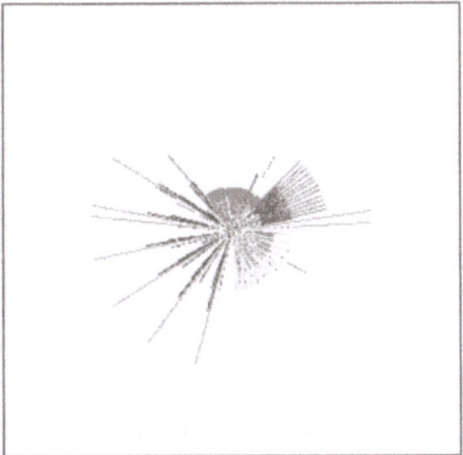

Figure 9.2. Nova (Plate 7).

the window in polar coordinates, with a radius given by the size of the allocation (&eventvalue), at a regular angular offset from the preceding value. Like pin-wheel, the graphic is drawn in a color that indicates the allocation type, based on the event code, and the display is animated at the rate at which memory allocations take place. An example screen image from nova is shown in Figure 9.2.

Like pinwheel, nova begins with an initialization section, followed by a loop that reads an event (again using NextEvent()) and draws a line at the appropriate angle and of the appropriate length.

```
procedure nova()
    local clear, xorg, yorg, radius, radians
    local arc, sector_units, fullcircle, erase, oldvalue
    initial gclear := 1
    erase := list(Sectors)
    fullcircle := 2 * &pi
    radians := 0
    sector_units := fullcircle / Sectors   # amount to advance
    xorg := WWidth() / 2
    yorg := WHeight() / 2
    radius := ((WHeight() < WWidth()) | WHeight()) / 2.0
    while NextEvent() do {
        put(erase, Value)
        oldvalue := get(erase)
        DrawLine(Background, xorg, yorg, \oldvalue * cos(radians) +
            xorg, oldvalue * sin(radians) + yorg)
```

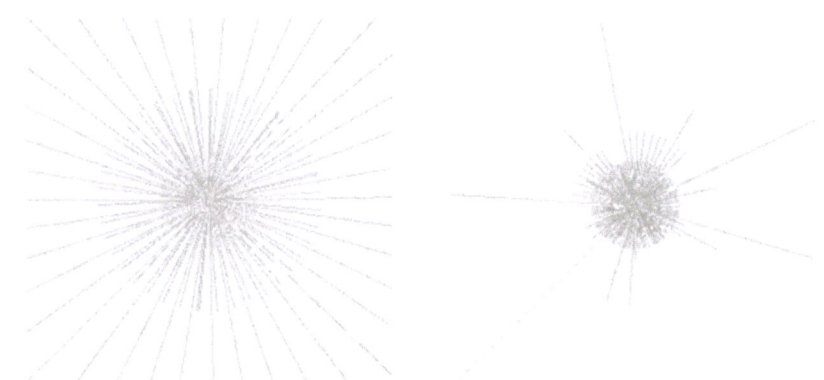

Figure 9.3. Frequent large allocations suggest a problem. The program runs twice as fast after a two-line change.

```
DrawLine(Binding, xorg, yorg, Value * cos(radians) +
    xorg, Value * sin(radians) + yorg)
radians +:= advance
}
end
```

The following example demonstrates how memory allocation monitors may be of practical use. A poetry-scrambling program submitted by a user produced the visual signature given in Figure 9.3 (left) when run under a tool using the nova metaphor. The wedge-shaped gap in Figure 9.3 (left) is present simply because the nova's sweep has not completed its first revolution. The program builds up very long lists by repeated concatenation, resulting in the frequent very large allocations shown in the figure. After changing two lines of code to replace a list concatenation with calls to Icon's put() function, the visual signature became normal, and program execution speed doubled (Figure 9.3, right).

## 9.2  Cumulative Allocation by Type

Visualizing individual allocation events is useful for understanding local phenomena, but an overall summary of memory allocation is also useful in understanding program behavior. The following code segment totals the amount of memory allocated in the program by data type, building a table of sums that is keyed by the allocation event codes for each type. The sums are cumulative, that is, garbage collections are not taken into consideration.

```
t := table(0)
while EvGet(AllocMask) do
    t[&eventcode] +:= &eventvalue
```

## 9.2.1  Animating a Bar Graph

The following procedure renders a list of nonnegative numbers in a window as a bar graph. Each bar in the graph is given a string name in a list called labels and is drawn using a color from a list of color contexts named colors; the indices of labels and colors match those of the list of numbers. The example can be improved in many ways; the scale can be labeled more clearly, the origins may be supplied as parameters instead of computed from the data, and so forth.

```
procedure bar_graph(L, labels, colors, scale)
    local height, x, y, i
    EraseArea()
    height := WHeight()
    bar_width := real(WWidth()) / *L
    WAttrib("label=Bar Graph, scale " || left(scale, 6))
    every i := 1 to *L do {
        x := (i − 1) * bar_width
        y := L[i] * scale
        FillRectangle(colors[i], x, height − y + 1, bar_width − 2, y)
        DrawString(x, 15, labels[i])
        }
end
```

If bar_graph is called frequently, such as every time an event occurs in an execution monitoring setting, the frequent window updates create a distracting amount of screen flicker. In such an animation, an incremental approach is more appropriate.

The following program updates a bar graph incrementally. The bar graph presents cumulative memory allocation by type. An example screen image from this animated bar chart is given in Figure 9.4.

The cumulative allocations are stored in list bars, in the order they appear on the screen. A parallel list of labels for each bar is maintained in labels; it is built from a table evs that maps event codes to their string names. The table is constructed by the standard evinit library procedure evsyms(). The mapping from event codes to screen position is maintained by the table typecode2bar. The animated bar graph scales itself as cumulative allocations increase.

```
&window := open("barmem","g") | stop("can't open window")
height := WHeight()
evs := evsyms()
```

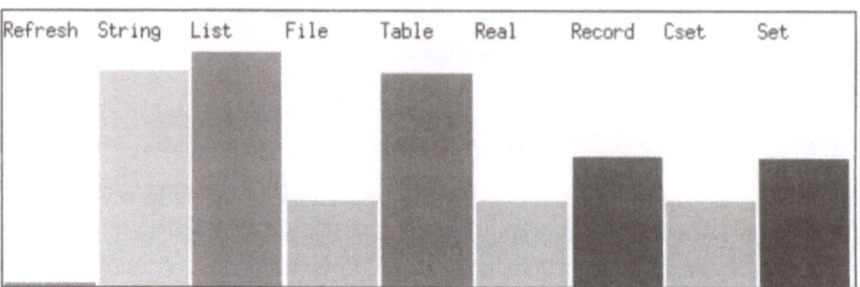

Figure 9.4. An animated bar graph.

```
typecode2bar := table()
bars := [ ]
labels := [ ]
scale := 4.0
```

The main loop requests an allocation event and calls procedure bar() to update the size of the bar that corresponds to the event. A new bar is created when a type's first allocation takes place. No screen space is devoted to types for which no allocation occurs. As each bar's label is obtained from the event names table evs, the event's E_ prefix is stripped by the string subscript [3:0].

```
while EvGet(AllocMask) do {
    if /event2bar[&eventcode] := *put(bars,0) then {
        put(labels, evs[&eventcode][3:0] | "?")
        put(Colors, contexts[&eventcode])
        }
    extent := bars[event2bar[&eventcode]] +:= &eventvalue
    extent *:= scale
    if extent > height − 20 then
        bar_graph(bars, labels, Colors, scale /:= 2)
    else
        bar(extent, Colors[t[&eventcode]], event2bar[&eventcode])
    }
```

The procedure bar() simply fills in a rectangle for the added space.

```
procedure bar(extent, Color, i)
    x := (i − 1) * bar_width
    y := height − extent + 1
    FillRectangle(Color, x, y, bar_width − 2 , &eventvalue * scale + 1)
end
```

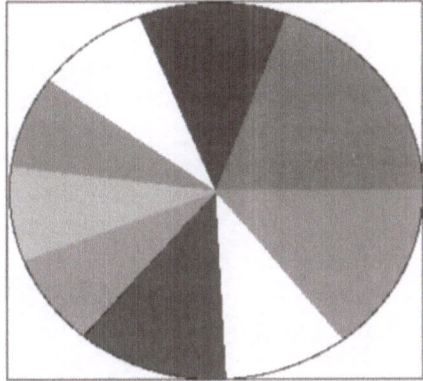

Figure 9.5. A pie chart.

### 9.2.2   Pie Charts

The following procedure draws a pie chart from a table shares in which each portion of the pie represents a key and their relative size is the key's table value. A parallel table colors of window bindings contains the color, grayscale, or texture that is used to distinguish each of the parts.

```
procedure draw_pie(shares, colors, sum, x, y, width, height)
    local start, fraction, k, path
    start := 0
    fraction := 360 * 64.0 / sum
    every k := key(shares) do {
        path := fraction * shares[k]
        FillArc(colors[k], x, y, width, height, start, path)
        start +:= path
        }
end
```

Unless the update rate is high, a visualization tool using this procedure can be animated by brute force by redrawing the entire image each time rather than incrementally. If the update rate is high, the chart might only be redrawn when a constituent's size changes by a significant amount, such as more than one percent of the total. A sample screen image from such a program is given in Figure 9.5.

## 9.3   Running Allocation by Type

In order to take garbage collections into account, the program must select E_Collect and E_EndCollect events. The E_Collect event is produced prior to

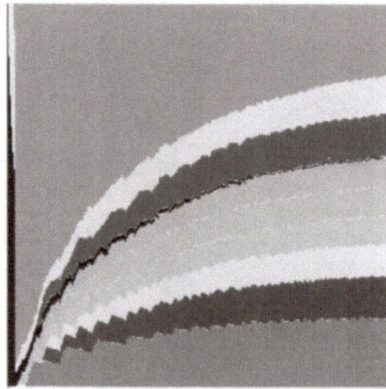

Figure 9.6. A memory allocation strip chart (Plate 7).

a garbage collection. The E_EndCollect event occurs after a garbage collection, and if it is selected, the monitoring instrumentation also produces (re)allocation events in between the E_Collect and E_EndCollect for the objects that survived the collection.

```
codes := AllocMask ++ E_Collect ++ E_EndCollect
t := table(0)
while EvGet(codes) do
    if &eventcode === E_Collect then t := table(0)
    else t[&eventcode] +:= &eventvalue
```

A more complex example of monitoring allocation by type is the following strip chart. It uses the same approach as the preceding example, but portrays a continuous animation in a window. In the following example, the y axis is used to show the proportions of memory used by all types. An example screen image from this program is given in Figure 9.6.

The program monitors all memory allocation and garbage collection information, maintains a table of running sums of memory by type, and draws each vertical line in the graph as a set of segments that are color-coded by type and whose length corresponds to the proportion of memory used by that type. An external library procedure, typebind(), is linked and used to provide the color encoding. typebind() returns a table whose keys are type allocation event codes and whose values are window bindings with foregrounds set to various colors; the table is stored in global variable Colors. Since colors vary from device to device, several palettes are available from typebind(), depending on the output device to be used. The global variable tallies refers to a table of sums of allocations keyed by type. Global variable heapsize stores the total amount of available memory. The event processing loop in procedure main() calls redraw() to update the window on each allocation and clears the window on garbage collection.

```
tallies := table(0.0)
heapsize := 0
every heapsize +:= keyword("regions", Monitored)
&window := open("MemoryType", "g")
Colors := typebind(&window, AllocMask)
mask := AllocMask ++ E_Collect
while EvGet(mask) do
    case &eventcode of {
        E_Collect: {
            EraseArea()
            tallies := table(0.0)
            }
        default: {
            tallies[&eventcode] +:= &eventvalue
            redraw()
            }
        }
```

The procedure redraw() updates the display when needed. Real arithmetic is used to minimize numeric errors in the mapping.

```
procedure redraw()
    static x
    initial x := 0
    start := 0
    every k := key(t) do {
        segment := WHeight() * real(tallies[k]) / heapsize)
        FillRectangle(Colors[k], x, start, 1, segment)
        start +:= segment
        }
    x := x + 1 % WWidth()
    EraseArea(x + 1, 0, 1)
end
```

It is possible to substantially improve on this trivial example; redundant calls and type conversions can be avoided, and many variations on the mapping from the problem space onto the image geometry are possible. In particular, it may be worth avoiding screen updates when the change to be reported is very small.

## 9.4  Survival Rates Across Collections

If a garbage collection reclaims only a small amount of storage, the TP may quickly run out of free memory and collect again. As the frequency of collections rises, overall system performance declines rapidly. This information can be obtained by selecting E_Collect and E_EndCollect events and reading TP's &storage keyword.

```
while EvGet(E_Collect) do {
    L := [ ]
    every put(L, keyword("storage", Monitored))
    EvGet(E_EndCollect)
    L2 := [ ]
    every put(L2, keyword("storage", Monitored))
    write("reclaimed ",integer(real(L[2] − L2[2]) / L[2] * 100),
        " percent of the string region")
    write("reclaimed ",integer(real(L[3] − L2[3]) / L[3] * 100),
        " percent of the block region")
}
```

# 10

# Monitoring String Scanning

As a descendant of SNOBOL4, Icon has a natural orientation towards text processing and includes a control structure devoted to that task. This chapter presents a brief overview of Icon's string scanning facilities and then gives example execution monitors that portray the target program's use of this control structure. The examples are themselves relatively simple, but demonstrate the framework's capabilities in this area and are suggestive of more advanced possibilities to be explored in this domain using the framework. Techniques for monitoring string scanning can be built by extending the techniques presented for monitoring procedure and operator activity in Chapter 7.

## 10.1   Overview of String Scanning

Icon's string scanning facility provides high-level text processing capabilities that free the programmer to think in terms of patterns in the text instead of character-by-character handling of indices and subscripts. String scanning operations work within the context of a string being scanned, the *subject*, and a current *position* of interest within that subject. Together, the subject and position form a *scanning environment* (Figure 10.1).

Figure 10.1. A string scanning environment.

The Icon expression

s ? *expr*

evaluates *expr* in a scanning environment that consists of subject s and an initial position of 1 (the beginning of the string). Scanning environments remain in effect inside any procedure calls within *expr*. Scanning environments may be nested; the outer scanning environment is saved and restored when the inner environment is entered and exited.

Operations on scanning environments include absolute and relative movement of the position as well as various forms of string and character set matching and searching. Relatively sophisticated parsing is performed by using these operators in conjunction with goal-directed evaluation and backtracking. In particular, the functions that change position within an environment, move() and tab(), undo their effects if they are resumed by backtracking.

## 10.2   String Scanning Events

Since a TP may suspend from and later resume a scanning environment, string scanning instrumentation includes a set of events for environment creation, suspension, resumption, failure, and removal, analogous to the events that occur as a result of procedure activity. Monitoring string scanning may entail the maintenance of a scanning environment tree using code similar to the procedure activity tree presented in Chapter 7.

In addition to these events, string scanning position changes result in the occurrence of E_Spos events. If the scanning position is restored by move() or tab() during backtracking, a second E_Spos event occurs.

Scanning environment activity including position change events can be selected by an EM using the library symbol ScanMask as the argument to EvGet(). In addition to ScanMask events, a string scanning monitor may be interested in calls to the built-in string scanning functions that comprise Icon's pattern matching primitives, such as find() and upto().

## 10.3     Absolute and Relative Position Changes

This section gives two simple EMs that present position change information with different emphases: (1) a view that portrays absolute position, and (2) a view that emphasizes relative position changes.

### 10.3.1     Visualizing Absolute Positions Within the Subject

String scanning operations move the position of interest within the subject forward or backward. Moving the position forward is common; moving the position backward is less common and usually is triggered by backtracking during goal-directed evaluation. It is useful to be able to observe when the position moves forward or backward and how large the changes in position are relative to the size of the string.

The following program displays an animated strip chart with subject lengths and position change information. For each position change event, the length of the subject is drawn down from the top and filled with two or three colors: a red segment indicates the current position or the number of characters already processed, while a white segment indicates the remainder of the string not yet processed. If backtracking has occurred, a gray segment in between the red and the white indicates the furthest forward that the scanning position has reached or the extent of the backtracking. A sample screen image is given in Figure 10.2.

The program starts with standard initialization code, including the creation of window bindings for drawing segments in red and gray. The width of each bar is determined by variable barwidth, and the number of pixels drawn per character in the various segments is specified in the variable scale.

The program's main loop requests position change events, and plots a segment on the window for each change. DrawRectangle() draws a black outline to indicate the size of the scanned subject; calls to FillRectangle() plot the red and

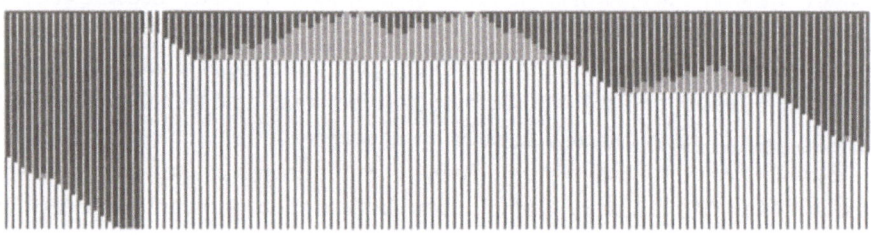

Figure 10.2. Absolute string position (Plate 6).

gray segments. A variable max holds the furthest position reached during scanning of a particular subject string; the gray segment is only drawn if backtracking has moved the position backwards into parts of the subject that have already been scanned.

```
while EvGet(E_Spos) do {
    s := keyword("subject", Monitored)
    position := &eventvalue
    if s == s_old then max <:= position
    else max := 1
    if *s > 0 then {
        DrawRectangle(x, 0, barwidth, scale * *s)
        FillRectangle(red, x, 0, barwidth, scale * (position − 1))
        if max > position then
            FillRectangle(gray, x, scale * (position − 1),
                barwidth, scale * (max − position))
        }
    x := (x + barwidth + 1) % WWidth()
    EraseArea((x + barwidth + 6) % WWidth(), 0, barwidth + 6)
    s_old := s
    }
```

This simple EM does not scale its output to fit the window; in the event a very long subject is scanned, output is clipped to window boundaries. An additional limitation is that backtracking information is not saved and restored for nested scanning environments.

## 10.3.2  Visualizing Relative Position Changes

By tracking relative position changes, backward motion is highlighted and large position changes are emphasized. The following EM plots relative position change as distance from the middle of the window, with forward position change

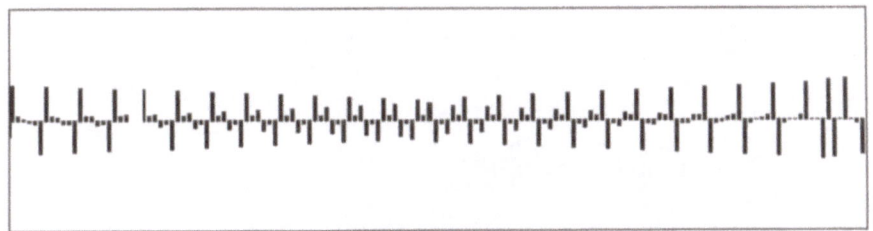

Figure 10.3. Relative string position.

going below the midpoint and backward position change going up from the midpoint. A sample screen image is shown in Figure 10.3.

After initialization, the main loop reads E_Spos events and uses the keyword() function to obtain the corresponding subject. If the subject is unchanged since the last event, the relative position change is noted. Like the previous example, this tool would provide more accurate information if it saved and restored the subject for nested scanning environments. The next section provides a method for doing so.

```
barwidth := 3
&window := open("pos", "g") | stop("can't open window")
x := 0
while EvGet(E_Spos) do {
    s := keyword("subject", Monitored)
    p := &eventvalue
    FillRectangle(x, WHeight() / 2, barwidth, 1)
    if s === s_old then
        if p > p_old then
            FillRectangle(x, WHeight() / 2, barwidth, p − p_old)
        else if p_old > p then
            FillRectangle(x, WHeight() / 2 − (p_old − p),
                barwidth, p_old − p)
    x := (x + barwidth + 1) % WWidth()
    EraseArea((x + barwidth + 6) % WWidth(), 0, barwidth + 6)
    s_old := s
    p_old := p
    }
```

## 10.4   The Scanning Environment Tree

Since scanning environments may be nested in much the same way as procedures, functions, and operators, it makes sense to use a tool similar to the Algae tool

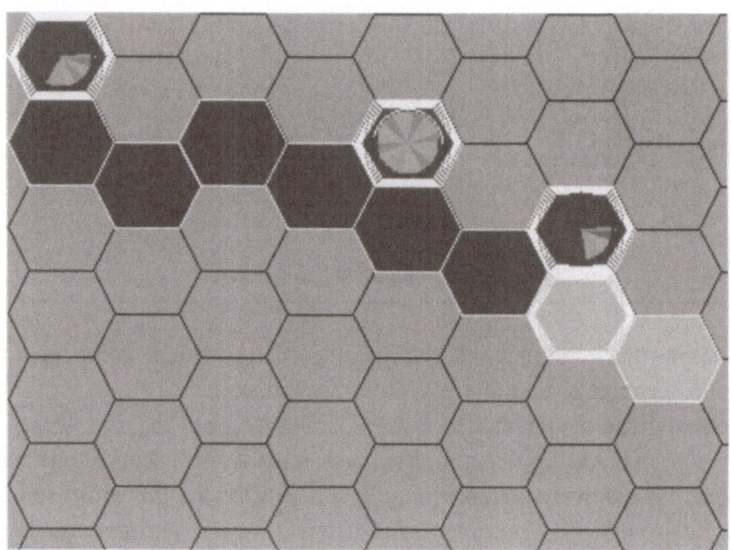

Figure 10.4. Scanning environment trees and operations (Plate 5).

presented in Chapter 8 to portray nested scanning environments. String scanning function and operator activity can be animated within the hexagons allocated by Algae for each scanning environment. This provides a detail view of scanning within the surrounding program execution context.

A modified version of Algae that displays string functions and operators encoded as colors is shown in Figure 10.4. The program uses the pinwheel metaphor from Chapter 9 to animate the sequence of operations independently within each scanning environment. Around the pinwheels' outside borders, circles are drawn in red, white, and gray segments to show current position and positional backtracking, similar to the absolute string positions example given earlier. The border around the pinwheel in the second column of Figure 10.4 is almost entirely dark (the grayscale depiction of red), indicating that the scanning position is almost to the end of the string, while the border around the pinwheel in the fourth column is only slightly dark above the three o'clock position, showing that the scanning position is still near the front of the scanned string.

In order to add this kind of detailed information about string scanning environments, extra fields are added to Algae's activation record type for the current scanning position, the farthest scanning position reached in the scanning environment, and the environment's pinwheel angle (expressed in units of 1/64th of a degree).

```
record activation(node, parent, children, row, column, color,
```

pos, maxpos, angle)

## 10.4.1  *Updating Position in the Current Scanning Environment*

Position change events are added to the event mask passed to evaltree(). The case
expression of the callback procedure for E_Spos events updates the current scanning environment's position fields, and draws red and gray arcs around the outside
of the hexagon to show position information. Global variables HexWidth and
HexHeight are used to determine the region inside the hexagon that is available
for drawing.

Note that a callback static variable, scanenv, is used rather than the current
activation (new), which can be a procedure, function, or operator called within the
current scanning environment. scanenv is maintained by code added to the case
expression branches of Algae's evaltree() callback procedure, described below.

```
case &eventvalue of {
    # ... other Algae case branches as given in Chapter 8
    E_Spos: {
        scanenv.pos := &eventvalue
        scanenv.maxpos <:= &eventvalue
        unit := fullcircle / *scanenv.node
        DrawArc(red, hexcolumn_x(scanenv.col) + 5,
            hexrow_y(scanenv.row, scanenv.col) + 5,
            HexWidth − 10, HexHeight − 10, 0,
            (&eventvalue − 1) * unit)
        if scanenv.maxpos > scanenv.pos then
            DrawArc(gray, hexcolumn_x(scanenv.col) + 5,
                hexrow_y(scanenv.row, scanenv.col) + 5,
                HexWidth − 10, HexHeight − 10,
                (&eventvalue − 1) * unit,
                (scanenv.maxpos − scanenv.pos) * unit)
        DrawArc(wwhite, hexcolumn_x(scanenv.col) + 5,
            hexrow_y(scanenv.row, scanenv.col) + 5,
            HexWidth − 10, HexHeight − 10,
            (scanenv.maxpos − 1) * unit,
            fullcircle − (scanenv.maxpos − 1) * unit)
    }
}
```

## 10.4.2  *Drawing Pinwheel Sectors for Scanning Functions*

The global table of colors is extended to map important string scanning functions
onto window bindings with foreground colors that indicate which function is being performed. Activity that involves these functions is captured by adding code

to the callback procedure's case expressions. The code for suspension events is shown here; similar code is added to the other cases.

```
!SuspCodes: {
    pinwheel(scanenv, \Colors[new.node])
    # ... rest of code for suspension events
    }
```

### 10.4.3  Pinwheels for Nested Scanning Environments

The added fields of an activation record are initialized whenever a new scanning environment event is received. The modified code looks like:

```
!CallCodes: {
    # ... code as given in Chapter 8
    if &eventcode === E_Snew then {
        new.pos := new.maxpos := 1
        new.angle := 0
        }
    }
```

The pinwheel drawing procedure from Chapter 9 is revised to take an activation record and a window binding with a foreground color to encode the string operation being performed, and draw a single sector in that foreground each time it is called.

```
procedure pinwheel(arecord, win)
    static full_circle, sector_units
    initial {
        full_circle := 360 * 64
        sector_units := full_circle / 16 # 16 sectors in the circle
        }
    radians := −dtor(arecord.angle / 64)
    x := hexcolumn_x(arecord.col) + 6
    y := hexrow_y(arecord.row, arecord.col) + 6
    width := HexWidth − 12
    height := HexHeight − 12
    center_x := x + width / 2
    center_y := y + height / 2
    FillArc(arecord.color, x, y, width, height,
        arecord.angle + sector_units, blank)
    FillArc(win, x, y, width, height, arecord.angle, sector_units)
    DrawLine(arecord.color, center_x, center_y,
        radius * cos(radians) + center_x,
        radius * sin(radians) + center_y)
    arecord.angle +:= sector_units
```

```
        arecord.angle %:= full_circle
end
```

## 10.5 Conclusions

String scanning is an important feature in Icon. In order to monitor it correctly, an EM must handle position changes as well as nested and suspended scanning environments. The extra attention required to monitor scanning correctly parallels the effort required to implement scanning correctly in the language.

Although string scanning is important, most programs use string scanning in extremely simple ways. Although detailed views will always be useful in debugging situations, in more general program understanding efforts, the information provided by literal text-oriented views of string scanning may be less useful than might be expected. A better approach may be to view string scanning within a larger context of program operation, such as the modified Algae example. It is not clear how to best monitor and visualize string scanning; this is still an open area for research.

# 11

# Monitoring Structure and Variable Usage

Previous chapters have demonstrated techniques for monitoring various aspects of program control and memory usage. Although some aspects of TP data usage are observable by means of memory allocation and garbage collection events, key aspects of program behavior are often characterized in terms of operations on program data, such as manipulations of program data structures or variable references.

This chapter presents techniques for monitoring data from both program-wide and narrower, variable-oriented viewpoints. Example EMs include list access monitors that show usage of Icon's built-in list data type on a program-wide scale, and variable reference monitors that show activity within individual procedure activations. There are many other ways to present data structure activity, and this is an open area of research. The examples in this chapter illustrate the capabilities and possible uses of the framework in this domain.

## 11.1 Visualizing Lists and List Accesses

On a program-wide scale, a tool that visualizes list activity is representative of techniques needed to monitor Icon's list, table, record, and set data types. Icon's list data type is used for a variety of purposes. Some programs use a few large lists, while other programs may use hundreds or thousands of small lists. Lists

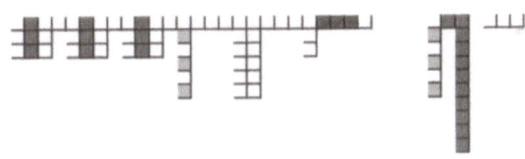

Figure 11.1. A list access monitor (Plate 8).

can change in size dynamically using both queue and stack operations, and they can also be accessed randomly similar to arrays in other languages.

The following EM portrays an overall view of list behavior in a TP. TP's lists are presented as a sequence of vertical bars, with each bar's length proportional to the size of the corresponding list. Vertical segments of the bars are color-coded by the types of the list elements. If all of a list's elements are of the same type, this forms a solid bar of that type's color; if a list is heterogeneous, its appearance is candy striped with the various colors of its elements' types. The horizontal position of a list's bar on the display is given by the list's serial number. A serial number is an integer associated with each list when it is created. Using serial numbers to determine screen position orders the lists from left to right by time of creation.

Queue, stack, and array-style random accesses are portrayed by changing the size of the bar (in the case of queue and stack accesses) or briefly painting a segment of the bar black and then redrawing it (in the case of random accesses). An example image from this program is given in Figure 11.1. Empty columns in this view indicate serial numbers at which no list has yet been created (on the far right) or lists that are empty or have been garbage collected (in the middle of the figure).

One of the key features of this program is a high degree of scalability necessary in order to accommodate programs with very large numbers of lists and yet present as much detail as screen space allows. In particular, if the number of lists is too large to fit in the window, the window is split into two rows and the number of vertical pixels per element is halved; this generalizes to $n$ rows of as few as one vertical pixel per list element. Figure 11.2 depicts a view in which the number of lists has caused a split into two rows. Figure 11.3 depicts a scaled image for a larger number (around 400) of lists requiring eight rows. Spaces in the figures again generally indicate empty or garbage-collected lists.

This scalability is achieved by maintaining a number of interdependent variables to describe the screen geometry. The window is divided into a matrix of size

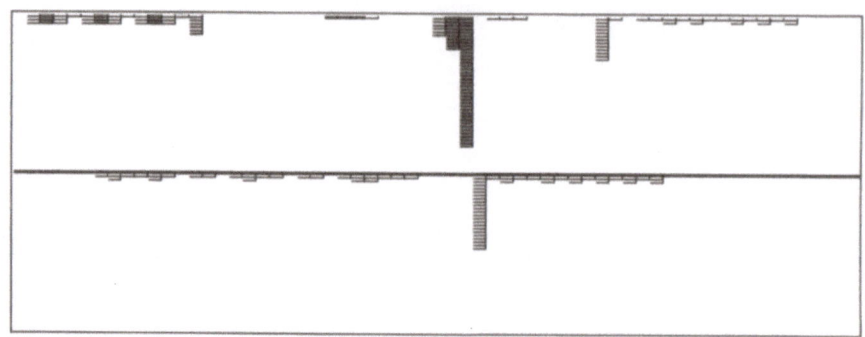

Figure 11.2. A moderate number of lists.

rows by cols corresponding to individual lists; each element of the matrix is in turn divided into vertical segments of height elem_height.

```
global
    rows,                   # number of rows of entire lists
    cols,                   # number of lists displayed per row
    elem_height             # height of an individual list element
```

In addition to this basic screen geometry, a count of the number of lists in TP is kept in number_active, and the mapping from lists to window (row,column) co-ordinates is maintained in table list_locations. The mapping from lists to window coordinates uses list serial numbers as keys, rather than list values themselves. If the EM retained references to the TP lists instead of their serial numbers, none of the TP lists could be reclaimed by garbage collection.

Procedure redraw() draws an entire picture of all the lists in the program. It uses the MT Icon function structure() to generate all the allocated structures in the program, and assigns each list a row and column. Each element of each list is then drawn by FillRectangle() in a color determined by the element's type by a call to objcolor().

```
procedure redraw()
    EraseArea()
    column_width := WWidth() / cols
    row_height := WHeight() / rows
    every i := 1 to rows − 1 do
        DrawLine(0, i * row_height, WWidth(), i * row_height)
    number_active := 0
    list_locations := table()
    every type(L := structure(Monitored)) == "list" do { # for every list
        number_active +:= 1
```

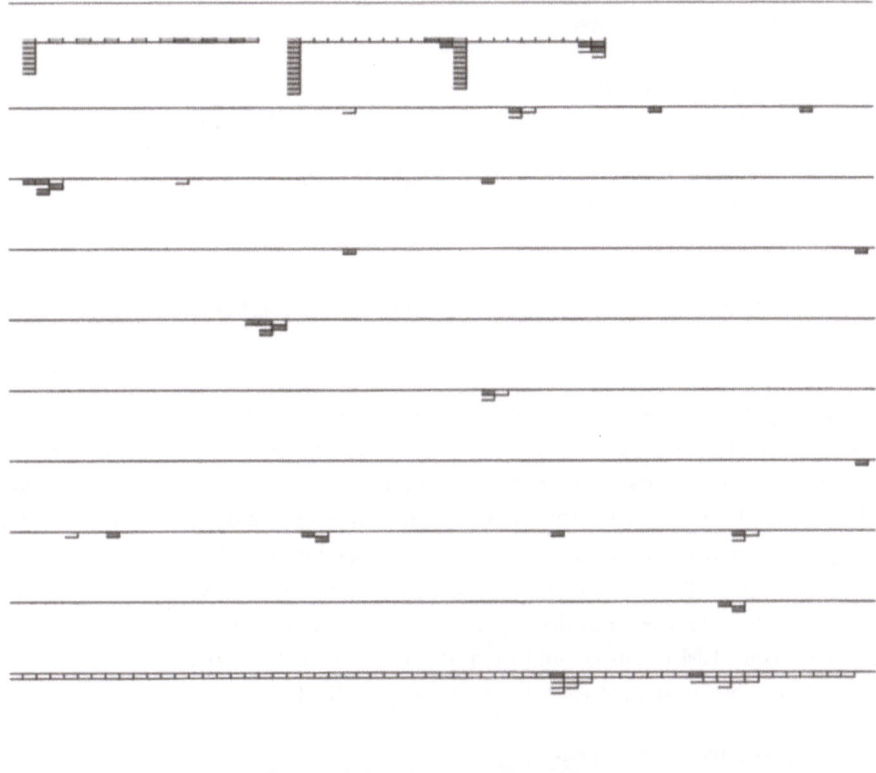

Figure 11.3. A large number of lists.

```
row := 1 + number_active / cols
col := number_active % cols
list_locations[serial(L)] := location(row, col)
every index := 1 to *L do
    FillRectangle(objcolor(L[index]), col * column_width,
        (row − 1) * row_height +
        (index − 1) * elem_height + 1,
        column_width, elem_height)
    }
end
```

Procedure redraw() is called whenever the scaling must be changed. The view it establishes can be updated incrementally for ordinary list construction and access by drawing one or more individual list elements with procedure plot(). plot() draws a rectangle, first with a black rectangle to highlight the access, and then with a rectangle of a specified color.

```
procedure plot(w, row, col, index, del)
    /del := 40
    x := col * column_width
    y := (row − 1) * row_height + (index − 1) * elem_height + 1
    if del > 0 then {
        FillRectangle(vblack, x, y, column_width, elem_height)
        WFlush(vblack)
        delay(del)
        }
    FillRectangle(w, x, y, column_width, elem_height)
end
```

The main loop fetches list events and updates by calling plot(). redraw() is called when the screen becomes full or the window size changes. One significant detail of list access monitoring is that a list access results in two events, one (E_Lref) with the list itself for an event value, and a second event (E_Lsub) with an integer event value that gives the index accessed within the list. EM saves the list value in the first event and uses it when the second is reported. Since the events come in pairs, TP does not do anything in between the two events, but after the second event, EM must use and then destroy its reference to the list or it might spuriously prevent the list from being garbage-collected.

```
while EvGet(ListMask) do
    case &eventcode of {
        E_Lref : L := &eventvalue
        E_Lsub : {
            index := &eventvalue
            if index < 0 then
                index +:= *L + 1
            loc := list_locations[serial(L)]
            plot(objcolor(L[index]),
                vertical(loc), horizontal(loc), index)
            L := &null
            }
        # ... other events handled similarly
        }
```

Although this example uses some sophistication to scale well to larger numbers of lists, it can be enhanced in various ways. For example, relaxing the direct mapping from serial number to screen location would allow screen space to be reclaimed whenever a list was garbage-collected. Another improvement would be to portray list operations in a visually distinct way instead of simply maintaining an accurate representation of the lists' contents.

## 11.2 Visualizing Heterogeneous Structures

Visualization poses challenges when structure types are treated in isolation, as in the preceding section. The challenges become harder when relationships between interconnected structures of different types are considered. Advanced languages such as Icon support *heterogeneous* structures: not just lists of strings and lists of lists, but lists of arbitrary elements that may be strings, lists, integers...whatever. For example, a hash table might implement both directions of a two-way table between a set of string names and integer values, containing keys of each type that map to values of the other type. When structures are heterogeneous, it is productive to consider visualizing them all together in the same image. In this case, the different methods of accessing data are what distinguish different data types. Since a single type may implement different interfaces with different access methods, this heterogeneity may actually be present when visualizing a single type. Icon lists, for example, offer array, stack, and queue access.

Both heterogeneous data values and heterogeneous access methods pose problems in debugging and in visualization. Textually naming elements several levels deep in a multi-level structure is tedious, and heterogeneous values only exacerbate the problem since the name used to access a sublevel may not be known until the type of the upper level is queried. More generally, characterizing the conditions of interest and distinguishing them from expected cases can be difficult or tedious, especially if the structure is complex.

The monitor described in this section is a heterogeneous structure visualizer, affectionately called the Structure Spy. This program displays relationships between arbitrary interconnected structures such as link lists, trees, and graphs. Nodes may be built from any Icon structure type, including lists, tables, sets, and records, which are color-coded. The Structure Spy is concerned only with interesting multilevel structures; structures that contain only references to nonstructures are ignored.

From the Spy's point of view, all structures are equivalent and the operations the Spy looks for are node creation and destruction, intracomponent changes, and splits and merges of connected components. Although structure references are unidirectional in Icon, all references are treated as bidirectional when determining the connected components.

As the target program runs and builds up structures, each connected component is depicted in a separate area in the window. Components' areas are subdivided into quarters and reallocated whenever more space is needed. Programs with a few large components look very different from programs with many small components. Figure 11.4 depicts a sample image of a single component consisting of interconnected nodes from a mixture of list and record data types.

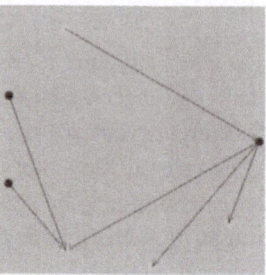

Figure 11.4. Heterogeneous structure visualization.

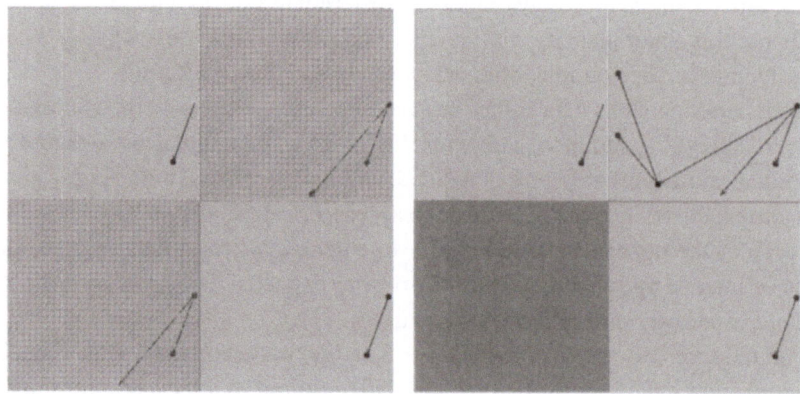

Figure 11.5. Before and after a merge of two components (Plate 9).

Merges of components happen when one large structure is inserted or linked to another. When this happens, the components being merged are briefly highlighted with light hashed lines, as shown in Figure 11.5 (left).

After a merger, the combined component is drawn in one of the two areas that were merged, and the other area is vacant until a new component is created and placed there. Figure 11.5 (right) shows the window after the merger is complete.

The source code for the Structure Spy is too lengthy to present in its complete form; we instead compare its implementation to the list monitor described above. The main() procedure uses a mask that asks for the union of the predefined sets of structure events, the assignment events, and the garbage-collection events. A table named Handlers maps event codes to associated procedures. For each event, the corresponding handler procedure is called via the table.

```
# initialization, including EvInit()
mask := StructMask ++ AssignMask ++ E_Collect ++ E_EndCollect
```

```
while EvGet(mask) {
  # ...
  (\(Handlers[&eventcode])) ()
  }
```

The event handler procedures examine the event value. If the structure operation is on a multilevel structure, its effect on the structure is classified (add a link,
delete a link, etc). The handler procedure for the list put() function is given below.
The event value after an E_Lput is the list after the element has been added to the
end; the newly added element on the end is thus &eventvalue[-1].

AddObjLink() inserts the new link into the Spy's model of the program structures; its parameters are source node, index or key, and destination node. ObjId
is a function that computes a string containing the type and serial number of the
event value for each event; these strings represent the object as a key in various
internal tables.

```
procedure ListPut()
  if IsObj(type(&eventvalue[-1]), 1) then {
    AddObjLink(ObjId(&eventvalue), *&eventvalue,
      ObjId(&eventvalue[-1]))
    }
end
```

The source code for the graphical layout is too long to present in detail here.
The layout is kept simple and is geared for scalably animating arbitrary programs'
behavior, rather than presenting attractive still shots of special cases. Components
are drawn in squares, and these squares are subdivided evenly into four pieces
when more space is needed for new components. The layout of an individual
component simply maps nodes around a circle to preserve the visibility of edges.

## 11.3    Monitoring Variable References

Monitoring structure accesses with techniques such as those described in the previous section is useful, but in many EMs, notably debuggers, data monitoring is
driven from the variables used in the program. We consider two examples of variable monitoring, one that visualizes all variables and one that identifies references
to specific variables of interest.

### 11.3.1    Assignment Events

One of the most common monitoring techniques is the observation of assignments, where the user is informed or monitoring code is executed whenever an

assignment to a particular variable or set of variables is made. The instrumentation reports an E_Assign event on each assignment. E_Assign has a string event value equivalent to calling name(v) on the assigned variable, suffixed by a *scope code*. The scope codes are

| Code | Scope |
|------|-------|
| "+" | global |
| ":" | static |
| "_" | local |
| "^" | parameter |

Statics, locals, and parameters are followed by the name of the procedure in which they are defined. For example, a local variable i in procedure main() would produce an E_Assign event value "i-main". Variable references to structure elements have no scope code.

For assignments to named variables and keywords, the name and scope are sufficient to perform reference detection; the name and scope may be augmented by procedure activity information in order to provide finer detail for local (and especially recursive local) variables. For assignments to structure elements, the event value cannot produce the name. A given structure element might be assigned by means of any of several variables that reference the structure. For this reason, reference detection techniques are different for named variables and for structure element variables.

## 11.3.2  Monitoring Variables by Name

Figure 11.6 shows a window image of a tool that displays the names and types of variables associated with procedure activations; the names are written in multiple columns in the case of a procedure with a larger number of variables. As its appearance indicates, the tool is an enlarged version of the Algae program from Chapter 8. The names of procedure parameters and local variables are displayed within each activation, drawn in a color that indicates the type of the variable. Colors are updated after each assignment. One useful extension to this tool is to show the values of integers. This is useful because integers are common, because they do not require much space, and because they are not heap-allocated and therefore do not appear in other data-oriented monitors.

The required modifications to Algae source code are omitted here for the sake of brevity; they are comparable to the extensions for string scanning given in the preceding chapter. The technique used is the monitoring of assignment events,

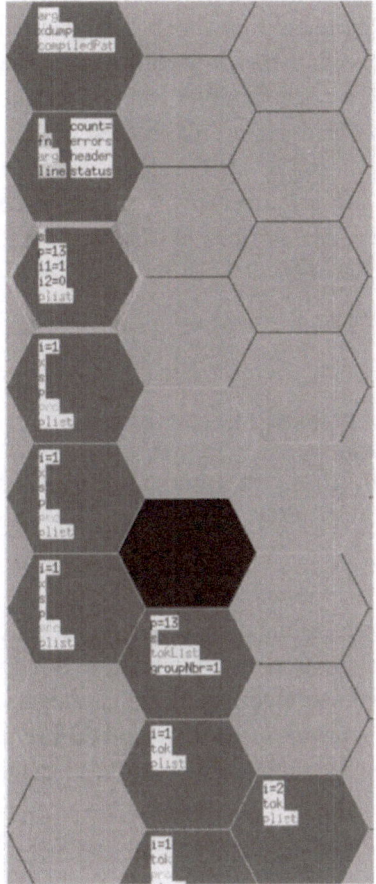

Figure 11.6. Monitoring variables in active procedures (Plate 5).

considering only those events whose scope code indicates either a local variable or parameter assignment.

The use of source text names creates serious spatial problems. Another reasonable way to extend this EM would be to modify it to use smaller rectangles for each variable and omit the names. Specific variables' names could be shown when the user clicks the mouse atop a particular variable.

### 11.3.3   Monitoring Individual Variables

A named variable is identified by its name and scope, or by its instantiating procedure activation if recursively created local variables are considered distinct. For such variables, reference detection is implemented using the E_Assign event values and some additional logic. Two examples below illustrate cases where (1) the EM acts on any assignment to a variable defined within a given procedure, and (2) the EM acts on assignments only within a specific activation record.

In the nonrecursive case, variables can be identified by their name and scope. A collection of variable names of interest might be stored in an Icon set ("trapped_variables" in the code below). Variable traps require selection of assignment events and maintenance of current procedure information using the evaltree() procedure, as described in Chapter 8 on following procedure activity. The correct invocation of evaltree() is:

evaltree(ProcMask ++ E_Assign, trap_callback, activation_record)

Procedure trap_callback() detects variable references with a set membership test.

```
procedure trap_callback(current_proc)
    if &eventcode === E_Assign then
        if member(trapped_variables, &eventvalue) then {
            # perform trap
            }
end
```

In some EM's, the handling of recursive procedure calls requires a more sophisticated form of variable trapping in which each individual local variable within each procedure activation record is treated as a distinct entity and can be trapped separately. This is relevant in recursive procedure calls. This form of trapping can be implemented by adding a field to the structure maintained for activation records:

record trapped_activation(p, parent, children, trapped_variables)

The variable reference detection is performed using this record type in an evaltree() invocation of the form:

evaltree(ProcMask ++ E_Assign, trap_callback, activation_record)

and replacing the line

if member(trapped_variables, &eventvalue) then {

in trap_callback() with the line

if member(new.trapped_variables, &eventvalue) then {

## 11.3.4  Detecting Structure Variable References

Icon structures have pointer semantics. Consequently, if two variables refer to the same structure, a trap on the name of an element of one of the variables will not catch an assignment using the other variable name. In the code

```
L1 := list(2)
L2 := L1
L2[1] := "foo"
```

a trap on variable L1[1] will not catch the assignment even though assignment is made to it. In order to trap structure elements, the information provided in assignment events need to be mapped down to the underlying structure.

Unfortunately, name(v) for a structure variable produces only a type code letter and a string image of the subscripting element. Without resorting to data-intrusive techniques such as altering the internal representation of Icon structures, monitors cannot tell from an assignment to an element which structure the element is in. Instead, monitors use the framework's extensive access to the program state.

Given the information E_Assign events provide about structure assignments, one way to trap structure elements is to check if a structure assignment *might* be a variable trap, and then compare all structures that might have been changed, after the assignment has been performed. In general, nonintrusive techniques for monitoring assignments are inefficient: this particular approach imposes a cost on structure variable assignments proportional to the number of trapped structure variables of the same type and index; if a large number of variables are to be trapped, data-intrusive techniques may be needed for performance reasons. An appropriate trapped variable technique has been developed for SNOBOL4 [31].

For every trapped structure variable, a triple consisting of the structure, the index or key, and the old value is maintained.

```
record trapped_structvar(struct, index, value)
```

These records are stored in a table, indexed by the string name that is reported by E_Assign when the variable is assigned.

Structure variable traps use not only E_Assign events, but also the E_Value events that are produced following the assignment. If the structure indexed by the key does not still equal the old value, the assignment has taken place. This technique is not capable of detecting assignments of the same value replacing itself in structures. The code is

```
codes := E_Assign ++ E_Value
while EvGet(codes) do
    case &eventcode of {
        E_Assign : {
            if match("T[" | "L[" | "R.", &eventvalue) then
                struct_asgn := trapped_structs[ &eventvalue ]
            else struct_asgn := &null
            }
        E_Value : {
            every tv := !\struct_asgn do
```

```
                if tv.struct [ tv.index ] ~=== tv.value then {
                    # the trapped structure element has been assigned
                    }
            }
        }
```

This technique works directly for tables and lists. It also works for record fields as long as the field is translated into its corresponding index for insertion into the trapped_structvar record.

# Part IV

# Visualization in the Programming Environment

# 12

# Monitor Coordination and Communication

As illustrated in the preceding chapters, MT Icon and its execution monitoring interface make it easy to develop new EMs. In this model, monitors are free to specialize in particular aspects of program execution, and the user selects the aspects to monitor in a given execution. When multiple EMs come into play, the selection of which EMs to use, the execution of those EMs, and their communication interface are the responsibility of a program called a monitor coordinator (MC).

This chapter presents monitor coordination as another domain within the scope of the exploratory program development features provided by the execution monitoring framework. After a general discussion of monitor coordinators, an example monitor coordinator is presented that implements a generalization of the *selective broadcast* communication paradigm advocated by Reiss [55]. Other paradigms of monitor coordination are possible within the framework. In addition, other generalizations of selective broadcast proposed in the literature may prove complementary to the one presented in this chapter [19].

## 12.1   Some Monitoring Configurations

MT Icon execution events are always reported to the parent program that loaded the TP being monitored. This means that the normal event reporting mechanism

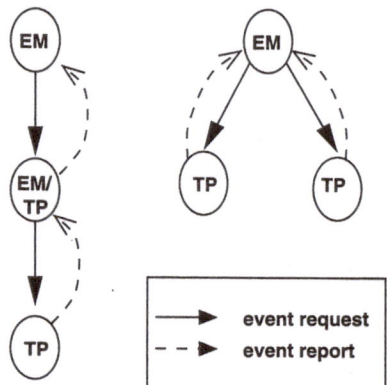

Figure 12.1. Monitoring a monitor; monitoring multiple TPs.

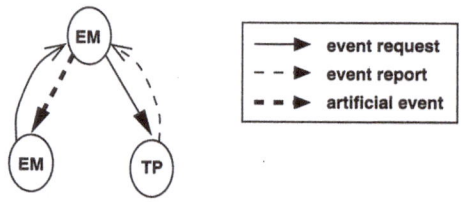

Figure 12.2. Forwarding events to an assistant.

handles simple relationships such as monitoring a monitor or monitoring multiple TPs (Figure 12.1).

On the other hand, the parental event report relationship means that if more than one EM is to monitor a TP, the TP's parent must provide other EMs with artificial copies of the TP events; MT Icon's event() function provides this service. Figure 12.2 depicts a parent EM that forwards TP events to an assisting EM.

Monitor coordinators are specialized EMs whose primary function is to forward events to other client EMs. A monitor coordinator is an event monitoring *kernel* that integrates and coordinates the operation of multiple standalone tools. By analogy to operating systems, the alternative to a kernel design would be a monolithic program execution monitor that integrates all operations into a single program.

Figure 12.3 depicts some relationships among MCs. Figure 12.3(a) is similar to Figure 12.2 and shows that an MC is just an execution monitor that forwards events. Figure 12.3(b) shows the main purpose for MCs, the execution of multiple EMs on a single TP. Figure 12.3(c) shows an MC monitoring an MC.

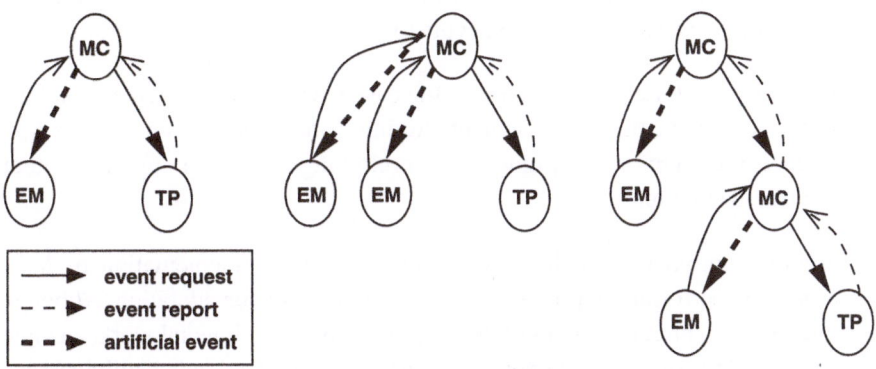

Figure 12.3. Monitor coordinators.

MC configurations and logic are generally limited to and revolve around parent-child relationships. For example, it is impossible to monitor events in a TP loaded and being monitored by another EM or MC unless that parent is configured to forward such events.

Since event reports also transfer control, MCs are also schedulers for EMs, relinquishing the CPU to them by forwarding events to them. In the simplest case, the MC forwards an event and waits for the EM to request another event before continuing; this scheduling is a form of cooperative multitasking. If the MC is the parent that loaded the EM in question, it can request event reports (such as clock ticks) from the EM in order to preempt its execution. Since MCs are special-purpose EMs, development of an efficient MC design falls within the scope of exploratory programming support provided by MT Icon.

## 12.2 Pros and Cons of the MC Approach

The three primary advantages of monitor coordinators are:

**Modularity** — With an MC, monitors can be developed independently of one another and of the MC itself; they can run as standalone monitors, directly loading and executing the program to be monitored. This allows monitors to be debugged separately and puts firewalls between monitors when they monitor the same program at the same time.

**Specialization** — Support for multiple monitors allows EMs to be written to observe very specific program behavior and still be used in a more general setting. This, in turn, reduces the burden of generality placed on EM authors. Specialization also simplifies the task of presenting information,

since each EM uses its own window and the user decides how much
attention and screen space to devote to each EM.

**Extensibility** — Extensibility refers to the ease with which new tools are added
to the visualization environment. Adding a new tool to run under a MC
does not require recompiling or even relinking the MC or any of the other
visualization tools.

Monitor coordinators do have disadvantages. The implementation of MCs
poses serious performance problems that require careful consideration. Although
unsuitable for exploratory monitor development and experimental work, a single
monolithic EM provides better performance than a MC that loads multiple EMs.

The primary problem with MCs is the number of context switches among
tasks; on some architectures, notably RISC architectures such as the Sun SPARC,
switching between coroutines is an expensive operation. Minimizing the number
of switches required must be a goal of most MC designs.

## 12.3    Eve: An Execution Monitor Coordinator

Eve is an example of an MC that allows the user to execute one or more EMs
selected from a list and forwards TP events to those EMs that the user selects.
The communication provided by Eve represents a generalization of the selective broadcast communications paradigm, because EMs may change the set of
events at any time during execution; in Reiss's FIELD system, tools can specify
the set of events they are interested in only when they are started. Unlike Forest's generalization of selective broadcast in which dynamic control is achieved
by placing a greater computational load on the coordinating message server, Eve
maintains an extremely simple message dispatch mechanism and passes policy
changes on to the TP by recomputing the TP's event mask whenever needed. By
suppressing events as early as possible, the higher performance required for execution monitoring is attained. This technique of continually minimizing the set of
events reported by the TP could be used in conjunction with a Forest-style policy
mechanism in the monitor coordinator, if that were desired.

Eve is a cooperative multitasking scheduler. Figure 12.4 shows an image of
Eve's control window. On the lefthand side are buttons that pause and terminate
TP execution and a slider that controls execution speed. The main area of the
window consists of a configurable list of EMs, and for each EM a set of buttons
allow the tool to be controlled during TP execution. In the figure, two EMs are
loaded and enabled. The source code for Eve is presented in Appendix B.

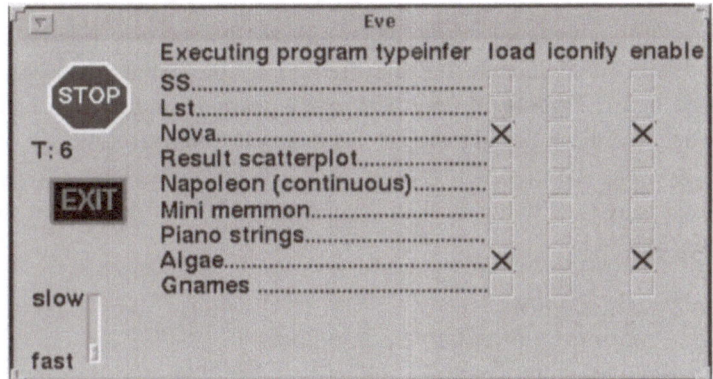

Figure 12.4. Eve's control window.

## 12.4    Writing EMs to Run Under Eve

Eve supplies events to client EMs using the standard **EvGet()** interface [24]. This section describes a few differences between the standalone interface and the Eve environment. Note that programs written for the Eve environment run without change or recompilation as standalone tools.

### 12.4.1    Client Environment

After each EM is loaded, Eve initializes it with references to its event source (the Eve program itself) and the TP. The former is necessary so that EMs yield control to Eve to obtain each event. The latter is provided so that the state of the TP may be examined or modified directly by all EMs. These references in the form of co-expression values are assigned to the keyword **&eventsource** and the global variable **Monitored**, respectively; the global variable **Monitored** is declared in each EM when it links to the **evinit** event monitoring library.

Since under Eve, &eventsource is *not* the TP, EMs should always use **Monitored** to inspect program state. For example, to inspect the name of the current source file in the executing program, an EM should call **keyword("file", Monitored)** rather than **keyword("file", &eventsource)**.

Aside from the fact that &eventsource is not **Monitored** under Eve, from a programmer's standpoint, Eve's operation is implicit. Just as monitoring does not inherently affect TP behavior (other than slowing execution), within the various EMs Eve's presence normally is not visible; the EM can call **EvGet()** as usual.

## 12.4.2   General-Purpose Artificial Events

Eve sends certain artificial events when directed by the user (in the Eve control window). These include the disable and enable events discussed above, E_Disable and E_Enable. A tool can pass a second parameter to EvGet() in order to receive these pseudo events, for example EvGet(mask, 1). When an E_Disable event is received, a tool is requested to disable itself. Tools that do not maintain any state between events can simply shut off their event stream by calling EvGet('', 1):

```
case &eventcode of {
    # ... more frequent events come first
    E_Disable: while EvGet('', 1) ~=== E_Enable
    }
```

Tools that require events in order to maintain internal consistency might at least skip their window output operations while they are disabled. An E_Enable event informs the tool that it should resume operation, updating its display first if necessary.

## 12.4.3   Monitor Communication Example

In addition to the use of artificial events for communication between Eve and other EMs, artificial events can be used by EMs to communicate with each other, using Eve as an intermediary. For example, a line number monitor such as the one shown in Figure 7.1 on page XX is more useful if the user can inquire about a section of interest in the line number graph and see the corresponding source text. This functionality can be built in to the line number monitor, but since many visualization tools can make use of such a service, it makes more sense to construct an EM to display source lines, and use virtual events to communicate requests for source code display from other EMs.

Communication using Eve starts with the definition of an artificial event code for use by the communicating EMs. Some of these codes such as E_Disable are defined in the standard library, but in general, EMs can use any artificial event codes that they agree upon. In this case, an event code, E_ALoc, is defined for artificial location display events. Communicating EMs also agree on the type and meaning of the associated event value. In this case, the associated event value is an integer encoding of a source line and column number, similar to that produced by E_Loc events.

The source code display EM is similar to other EMs, except that it is not interested in TP events, but only in E_ALoc events. Its main loop is

```
while EvGet('', 1) do
    if &eventcode === E_ALoc then {
        # process requests for source code display
    }
```

Any EM that wishes to request source location display services sends an E_ALoc event to Eve. Eve then broadcasts this event to those tools that requested artificial event reports. The code to send a location request event to Eve from within an EM is

```
loc := location(line, column)
event(E_ALoc, loc, &eventsource)
```

## 12.5   Eve in Operation

This section describes the primary techniques employed in Eve to obtain good performance. The key ideas are to filter events at the source and to precompute the set of EMs to which each event code is distributed.

Different EMs require different kinds of events. After obtaining a list of client EMs to execute, Eve loads each client. It then activates each EM for the first time; when the EM completes its initialization, it calls **EvGet()**, passing Eve an event mask.

### 12.5.1   Computation of the Minimal Event Set

Each time an EM requests its next event report from Eve, it transmits a cset event mask indicating which events it is interested in. Eve could simply request all events from the TP, and forward event reports to each EM based on its current mask. The interpreter runtime system is instrumented with so many events that this brute-force approach is too slow in practice. In order to minimize the cost of monitoring, Eve asks the TP for the smallest set of events required to satisfy the EMs.

From the event masks of all EMs, Eve computes the union and uses this cset to specify events from the TP. The code for this union calculation is

```
unioncset := ''
every monitor := !clients do
    if monitor.enabled === E_Enable then
        unioncset ++:= monitor.mask
```

Every EM can potentially change its event mask every time it requests an event. Constant recomputation of the union mask would be unacceptably expensive. Fortunately, most tools call **EvGet()** with the same event mask cset over and over again. Eve does not recompute the union event mask unless an EM's event mask changes from the EM's preceding event request.

## 12.5.2    The Event Code Table

The minimal event set described above greatly reduces the number of events actually reported from the TP. When an event report is received from the TP, Eve dispatches the report to those EMs that requested events of that type. The larger the number of EMs running, and the more specialized the EMs are, the smaller the percentage of EMs that typically are interested in any given event.

Eve could simply test the event code with each EM's cset mask with a call any(mask, &eventcode). This test is fast, but performing the test for each EM is inefficient when the number of EMs is large and the percentage of EMs interested in most events is small. Instead, the list of EMs interested in each  event code is precomputed as the union mask is constructed. These lists are stored in a table indexed by the event code. Then, after each event is received, a single table lookup suffices to supply the list of interested EMs. For each enabled monitor, the code for union mask computation is augmented with:

```
every c := !monitor.mask do {
    /EventCodeTable[c] := [ ]
    put(EventCodeTable[c], monitor)
    }
```

## 12.5.3    Event Handling

Eve requests three types of events whether or not any client EM has requested them: E_Tick, E_MXevent, and E_Error. Eve uses these events to provide basic services while execution is taking place; since these events occur relatively infrequently, they do not impose a great deal of overhead.

E_Tick events allow Eve to maintain a simple execution clock on the control panel. E_MXevent events allow Eve to receive user input (such as a change in the slider that controls the rate of execution) in its control panel. E_Error events allow Eve to handle runtime errors in the TP and notify the user when they occur, allowing errors to be converted to expression failure at the user's discretion. As in the Structure Spy in Chapter 11, handlers for events are called through a global table indexed by event code, allowing for easy extension.

## 12.5.4    Eve's Main Loop

Eve's main loop activates the TP to obtain an event report, and then dispatches the report to each EM whose mask includes the event code. Since this loop is central to the performance of the overall system, it is coded carefully. Event dispatching to client EMs costs one table lookup plus a number of operations performed for each EM that is interested in the event—EMs for which an event is of no interest do not add processing time for that event. The code for Eve's main loop is:

```
while EvGet(unioncset) do {
    #
    # Call Eve's own handler for this event, if there is one.
    #
    (\ EveHandlers[&eventcode]) ()
    #
    # Forward the event to those EMs that want it.
    #
    every monitor := !EventCodeTable[&eventcode] do
        if C := event( , , monitor.prog) then {
            if C ~=== monitor.mask then {
                while type(C) ~== "cset" do {
                    #
                    # The EM has raised a signal; pass it on, then
                    # return to the client to get its next event request.
                    #
                    broadcast(C, monitor)
                    if not (C := event( , , monitor.prog)) then {
                        unschedule(monitor)
                        break next
                        }
                    }
                if monitor.mask ~===:= C then
                    computeUnionMask()
                }
            }
        else
            unschedule(monitor)
        # if the slider is not zero, insert delay time
    }
```

## 12.6   Interactive Error Conversion

Normally, execution terminates when a runtime error occurs. Icon supports a feature called *error conversion* that allows errors to be converted into expression failure. Error conversion can be turned on and off by the source program by assigning an integer to the keyword &error. &error indicates the number of errors to convert to failure before terminating the program; on each error the value of

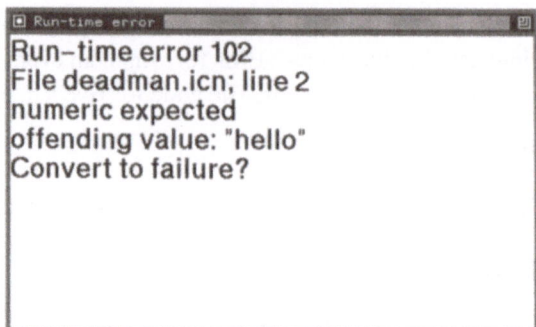

Figure 12.5. Eve's interactive error converter.

&error is decremented and if it reaches zero, the program terminates. A program can effectively specify that all errors should be converted by setting &error to a small negative integer. The mechanism is limited in that it does not allow the user or the program to inspect the situation and determine whether error conversion is appropriate: error conversion is either on or it is off.

Eve catches runtime errors in the TP and allows the user to decide whether to terminate execution or convert the error into expression failure and continue execution (Figure 12.5).

An E_Error event occurs upon a runtime error. A monitor that requests E_Error events is given control before the error is resolved. Eve requests these events, presents the user with the error, and asks for an appropriate action. The code in Eve that does interactive error conversion is:

```
procedure eveError()
    win := open("Runtime error " || &eventvalue, "g")
    write(win, "Runtime error ", &eventvalue)
    write(win, "File ", keyword("file", Monitored),
        "; line ", keyword("line", Monitored))
    write(win, keyword("errortext", Monitored))
    writes(win, "Convert to failure? ")
    if read(win)=="y" then
        keyword("error", Monitored) := 1
    close(win)
end
```

# 13
# Performance

In the absence of specialized hardware support, monitoring imposes significant performance overhead on TP execution. In practice, the user of the system usually is unable to observe execution behavior in any detail at the rate at which it is generated by the monitoring system, and must frequently stop or slow down execution in order to inspect details. Similarly, the more sophisticated the execution monitor's analysis of execution behavior, the more overall execution speed directly relates to time spent in the monitor. In light of these facts, performance considerations for the monitoring framework are not as important as the quality and utility of the information provided by EMs.

Nevertheless, many of the systems discussed in Chapter 2 are reported to experience performance problems, especially tied to the rate at which information is extracted from the target program. Execution monitoring is useful only if the performance of the implementation is fast enough so that the system can be applied successfully to medium and large programs and solve real-world problems. Empirically, the framework developed for monitoring Icon programs meets this criterion.

The purpose of this chapter is to measure the performance overhead associated with monitoring in MT Icon. Since the general execution model may be relevant to the monitoring of other high-level languages, costs are provided for separable components such as the implementation of multitasking and the interpreter instrumentation. The evaluation is concerned primarily with time measures, rather than space requirements; space has not been an issue in practice.

The performance results provided in this chapter start with baseline measurements of the cost of multitasking support and instrumentation, followed by measurements of the relative costs of monitoring different types of language events. The chapter concludes with a note on the effect of CPU type upon the cost of monitoring, and a discussion of the costs incurred by monitor coordinators.

## 13.1   Costs of Multitasking and of Interpreter Instrumentation

The reference point for measurements presented in this chapter is the Version 8.10 Icon interpreter, which can be conditionally compiled with no tasking or monitoring support, with multitasking, or with multitasking and monitoring support. The performance results are consistent with those seen on current platforms running Icon version 9.3, with the exception that Sun has added hardware support for lightweight context switches on recent generation Sparc processors, which vastly improves monitor performance under the Icon framework.

The first cost to be considered is that of the multitasking implementation employed by MT Icon. The implementation is optimized for detailed monitoring in which many event reports take place, and task switching is therefore extremely frequent. In order to minimize the cost of the task switch, an extra memory reference is imposed when accessing task-specific global variables in the runtime system. The overhead on these extra memory references is insignificant compared with overall interpreter execution costs.

Timings for the Icon benchmark suite [23] run on a Sun Sparcstation IPX under the Icon interpreter compiled without multitasking and then with multitasking support are shown in the two leftmost columns of Figure 13.1. The remaining columns are discussed below. Generally, the benchmarks' execution differences under Icon and MT Icon are small enough to fall within the margins of error in the measurements due to variations in machine load.

| TP | Icon | MT Icon | MT Icon with events | ... with VM |
|---:|---:|---:|---:|---:|
| conc | 5.5 | 5.7 | 8.9 | 10.2 |
| deal | 6.6 | 6.6 | 8.0 | 9.1 |
| ipxref | 1.3 | 1.4 | 2.1 | 2.2 |
| queens | 8.1 | 8.2 | 12.4 | 13.2 |
| rsg | 8.2 | 8.1 | 11.5 | 12.8 |

Figure 13.1. MT Icon benchmark timings (seconds).

In addition to multitasking, execution monitoring depends on the presence of instrumentation added inline to the interpreter and runtime system code under conditional compilation. When compiled with instrumentation, the interpreter performs tests to determine whether to report each event, even if monitoring is not being performed. The column of Figure 13.1 labeled "MT Icon with events" gives Icon benchmark suite timings using an interpreter built with monitoring instrumentation. Since instrumentation of virtual machine instructions imposes a significant cost all by itself, the figures in the rightmost column show timings with virtual machine instructions included. Generally, the presence of pervasive instrumentation increases execution time 30 to 50 percent even when it is not used.

This measure is independent of the co-expression model and the use of independently written and translated Icon programs as monitors. The cost of instrumentation would be incurred even if the monitoring system, including visualization code, were tightly integrated into the Icon interpeter itself.

## 13.2  Varying Costs of Monitoring Language Features

Some classes of events are much more costly to monitor than others. This is roughly proportional to the frequency with which an event occurs. For example, garbage-collection events occur very rarely, so it costs very little to monitor them. Line number changes are far more frequent; virtual machine instructions are the most common of all. The classes of events covered are memory allocations, assignments, type conversions, structure accesses, procedure activity, built-in function activity, operator activity, string scanning activity, program source code location changes, and virtual machine instruction execution.

Figure 13.2 gives benchmark suite event counts in the leftmost column, followed by percentages for each of the major categories of events, and Figure 13.3 gives execution times for monitors that request those events but do no computation of their own. The timings are generally proportional to the amount of work actually performed by the computation, and not a direct function of any particular class of events. Generally, however, the more events monitored, the greater the slowdown imposed by monitoring. Comparison of Figures 13.1 and 13.3 shows that on a Sparc, monitoring typically imposes an overhead of one order of magnitude for infrequent event categories, or two orders of magnitude for virtual machine instructions, compared with execution under the standard Icon interpreter. Computations performed by the EM or EMs as they process events further slow TP execution.

With the exception of garbage collections, there are 1.18 events per virtual machine instruction on average, typically ranging from one (the virtual machine

|        | total # | alc | asn | cnv  | struc | proc | fun | op   | scan | loc  | VM   |
|--------|---------|-----|-----|------|-------|------|-----|------|------|------|------|
| conc   | 3782971 | 1.7 | 4.9 | 20.5 | 0.2   | 0.2  | 9.1 | 8.8  | 1.8  | 8.2  | 44.6 |
| deal   | 1963019 | 3.2 | 5.7 | 26.5 | 1.4   | 1.1  | 2.1 | 12.8 | 0    | 7.9  | 34.7 |
| ipxref | 1044476 | 0.6 | 1.7 | 21.1 | 3.4   | 0.5  | 1.3 | 18.9 | 0    | 8.7  | 43.8 |
| queens | 6835489 | 0.1 | 4.0 | 29.9 | 4.3   | 0.2  | 0   | 18.0 | 0    | 8.0  | 35.3 |
| rsg    | 5367792 | 0.9 | 2.7 | 4.0  | 3.7   | 0    | 3.7 | 13.5 | 0    | 10.0 | 61.5 |

Figure 13.2. Total event counts and percent of events in each category.

|        | alc  | asn   | cnv   | struc | proc | fun   | op    | scan | loc   | VM    |
|--------|------|-------|-------|-------|------|-------|-------|------|-------|-------|
| conc   | 33.2 | 72.4  | 225.3 | 14.6  | 14.5 | 107.1 | 107.8 | 34.7 | 114.7 | 386.2 |
| deal   | 52.2 | 47.8  | 153.3 | 17.9  | 16.3 | 21.6  | 80.6  | 10.0 | 71.8  | 184.1 |
| ipxref | 4.5  | 8.1   | 63.4  | 12.4  | 4.2  | 6.5   | 56.1  | 2.6  | 41.4  | 102.6 |
| queens | 19.2 | 108.7 | 584.8 | 101.4 | 21.5 | 16.1  | 362.4 | 16.0 | 208.7 | 534.8 |
| rsg    | 29.8 | 59.8  | 74.7  | 71.9  | 16.0 | 72.9  | 205.1 | 15.5 | 214.5 | 761.7 |

Figure 13.3. Execution times for no-op monitors by category (seconds).

instruction event itself) to around twelve. The number of events that occur per virtual machine instruction is not strictly bounded, since a garbage collection can result in a number of events proportional to the number of data objects that survive collection in the block region.

For each virtual machine instruction in the TP, an EM potentially receives several event reports resulting in arbitrarily lengthy computations on its part. Since event reporting is built around the Icon co-expression context switch, the CPU-dependent speed of the context switch operation compared with normal program activities is important in determining the cost of using a multitasking model of execution monitoring instead of a one-process model. Figure 13.4 compares timings of ordinary operations, context switches, and event reporting on the Sun Sparcstation IPX and an Intel 486 processor. The figures are the average from one million executions of each operation. The first three columns give timings for the null operation, integer addition, and procedure call. The fourth column times the Icon co-expression context switch, while the fifth column times the event reporting mechanism, including its context switch.

The first and third rows report timings taken using Icon's built-in timing mechanism, while the second and fourth rows give times observed by the UNIX shell time command. Although the Sparcstation performs almost twice as fast as the i486 on normal computations, its advantage is greatly reduced for execution monitoring because its context switch is very slow—the context switch executes a software trap that flushes register windows to memory. When this system time is

| CPU | no-op | i + j | p(x) | @x | event()...EvGet() |
|---|---|---|---|---|---|
| Sparc &time | 10.4 | 38.8 | 33.6 | 97.5 | 277.8 |
| Sparc u+s time | 10.2+0.1 | 39.4+0.4 | 33.6+0.2 | 79.5+93.5 | 222.0+113.0 |
| i486/33 &time | 19.5 | 63.8 | 58.5 | 78.0 | 363.7 |
| i486/33 u+s time | 11.7+0.2 | 38.2+0.2 | 34.9+0.1 | 46.5+0.1 | 235.2+1.6 |

Figure 13.4. Costs of various operations (microseconds, average).

taken into account (adding the two figures given in each column of the second and fourth rows), the i486 outperforms the Sparc IPX by a factor of 4 for the co-expression context switch, and by roughly 50 percent on the event reporting mechanism. Of course, the Sparc's performance advantage on the rest of the TP and EM execution translates into faster execution overall.

## 13.3    Limitations of Graphics Hardware and Software

Experience has shown that in many program visualization applications, the window system software is not able to perform window output at the rate at which it is produced by an EM; this is observed when monitors written using asynchronous window system calls complete execution noticeably before animation stops in the monitor window. For such applications, writing EMs in Icon instead of a lower-level language does not cost as much in terms of performance as might be expected. In contrast, MT Icon is least suitable for EMs with complex graphics requiring significant numeric computation, because such applications' performance is less likely to be limited by window system capabilities and because Icon is not oriented towards numeric applications.

## 13.4    Cost Incurred by Monitor Coordinators

Although MCs offer great flexibility, the use of an MC to execute multiple EMs instead of writing a single monolithic EM imposes additional overhead, primarily increasing the number of task switches required. The MC Eve can be used to illustrate this cost.

In the worst case, all EMs request a report for every event. Under Eve, if there are N tools, then there are 2 * N + 2 task switches per event report. A monolithic EM would incur only two switches per event report, from TP to EM, and from EM to TP. Eve therefore imposes 2 * N additional switches in the worst case.

In the best case, the event masks are disjoint and only one EM is interested in any event to be reported. In this case, Eve incurs four task switches per event report—twice as many as in the monolithic case. Since users typically employ multiple EMs to provide information about a variety of aspects of program behavior, the expected normal case is closer to this best case behavior than the worst case in which the EMs are all observing the same events.

# 14

# Conclusions and Future Work

MT Icon and its instrumentation provide a framework in which it is possible to take a program monitoring idea from conception to implementation in a short period of time. The primary contribution in this framework is the exploitation of coroutines and dynamic loading to provide EMs with program state information at the source level instead of at the machine level.

## 14.1 Successes of the Framework

The framework demonstrates the viability of:

- exploratory development of execution monitors, given suitable language support,

- a synchronous task model for the monitoring of programs written in high-level languages,

- application of monitors developed under the framework to obtain useful performance tuning information.

MT Icon's execution monitoring interface has proven simple enough to be programmed even by novice Icon programmers. In one semester, students with no prior Icon programming experience were able to use the framework in a university course to construct sophisticated program visualization tools. Expert users can construct experimental EMs in hours instead of days.

Exploratory monitor programming is of limited usefulness if it does not scale up to accommodate the development of larger, full-featured monitoring services. MT Icon allows the execution of multiple EMs on a single TP using a monitor coordinator as an attractive alternative to monolithic, all-encompassing tools such as traditional debuggers and profilers. Performance degrades gracefully as tools are added.

Dynamic loading and synchronous, shared address space tasks have proven to be a robust model in which TP and EMs can coexist. Task switching between TPs and EMs provides acceptable performance while minimizing the impact of monitoring upon the behavior of the TP.

The implementation of dynamic loading and multitasking in MT Icon builds upon Icon's implementation of co-expressions. The execution monitoring framework is therefore portable to most of the platforms that Icon runs on with the exception of personal computers with small memory sizes. The system has been run on a variety of UNIX platforms as well as Windows and OS/2. Many of the more powerful EMs make extensive use of Icon's graphics facilities; use of graphics is a greater portability limitation than MT Icon and the execution monitoring interface.

The Alamo Icon framework has been used to implement a variety of profiling tools for tuning performance, such as tools that count the number times a given line or given procedure has been executed. Of particular interest are language-specific tools that profile behavior that is not related directly to the program source code, but rather takes place in the runtime system, such as garbage collection or type conversion. Such costs may not be readily apparent to a programmer writing or reading the code.

One such profiler simply indicates in a small window whenever a garbage collection takes place. For normal programs, this monitor imposes little overhead and is unobtrusive, while programs that are exhibiting thrashing heap behavior flash repeatedly, drawing attention to the problem. Upon observing such behavior, the user may be able to adjust heap size parameters so that thrashing does not occur in future executions.

A more sophisticated profiler cross references type conversion information with program source locations and applies simple heuristics to select locations where frequent conversions are likely to be unnecessary or redundant. The user then can manually inspect the locations found to determine whether a simple modification can eliminate the conversions. The redundant conversions profiler has resulted in speedups of 0 to 15 percent on real programs, with useful results in programs written both by novice and expert users.

In addition to profiling tools, program tuning often results from the observation of behavior presented by more general EMs. For example, inefficient structure manipulations can frequently be inferred by observing allocation patterns or structure access activity, as in the nova tool example in Chapter 9.

Success in target program tuning suggests the related issue of language implementation tuning. MT Icon's execution monitoring framework was not built with the objective of providing information for improving the implementation. Nevertheless, prior research in the monitoring and visualization of memory usage led to improved allocation heuristics [30], and observation of EMs under MT Icon also suggested improvements to the implementation. For example, monitoring of list creation events led to a change in list concatenation with the result that it is faster and allocates less space than before.

Instrumentation also can find problems in the implementation. Modifications to the implementation during the construction of the Icon compiler at one point introduced a bug into the implementation of the built-in string analysis function many(). The bug allowed many() to produce string indices beyond the bounds of the subject string. The bug was observed in a string scanning EM, where position events appeared past the end of the subject string.

## 14.2    Limitations of the Framework

Although the framework addresses the construction of monitors for a broad spectrum of program behavior, the techniques it uses are of limited applicability to other languages, and the ability to monitor implementation behavior does not extend into the realm of observing activity during garbage collection. In addition, there are inherent limitations in the use of non-intrusive monitoring techniques: some kinds of debugging require intrusion into the target program, and the framework is not oriented towards intrusive techniques.

The approach to execution monitoring presented here is not applicable to programming languages and systems in which the implementor of the execution monitoring facilities does not "own" the implementation of the language. Beyond access to source code, instrumentation of a language runtime system generally requires intimate knowledge of the implementation and represents a major investment of effort. Because instrumentation is spread throughout the code, it poses added maintenance problems in the implementation and must be added to the primary source if it is to remain functional in future language updates and versions.

The technique of capturing program behavior via runtime system instrumentation is not appropriate for low-level compiled languages, where instrumentation is more appropriately embedded in generated code via a preprocessor or compiler modifications. Instrumentation of an interpreter is generally simpler and easier than modifying a compiler code generator.

MT Icon's dynamically loaded coroutines do not have ready equivalents in most other languages and would have to be added, as they were to Icon, before the exploratory execution monitor development provided by MT Icon can be realized. The implementation of a portable dynamic loading mechanism was much simpler for an interpreter than would be the case for a compiled language. In some cases, notably Smalltalk, the language has the requisite features, but the implementation may require added features such as separately collected heap spaces before EMs can execute without interfering with TP behavior.

Another limitation of the framework is in the area of garbage-collection monitoring. The MemMon system is able to provide very detailed information about Icon's marking and compaction algorithms through a file-based event stream [30]. This information has proven useful in practice, but there is no way to safely report events during a garbage collection in MT Icon. An event report causes transfer of control and execution in an EM. During a garbage collection, TP data may not be in a valid format and if an EM were free to inspect it, system failure would result.

This is one inherent penalty in the one-process and thread models in which EMs directly access TP data through pointers. Since this limits the monitoring of implementation behavior, rather than TP behavior, it is not an unacceptable loss. MT Icon does provide events that show when a collection occurs, and what values survived the collection, but no more. If the garbage collection algorithm itself is under study, a two-process model or file-based monitoring system should be employed rather than the MT Icon task model. More fundamentally, in such cases the memory must be traversed at the implementation level, rather than the source level as in MT Icon.

## 14.3    Enhancements and Future Directions

The execution monitoring framework for Icon was motivated by a desire to explore new types of execution monitors, particularly program visualization tools. The framework is an enabling technology, and its success should result in the development of various experimental monitoring tools. In addition, some general problems in execution monitoring have been observed that further work may mitigate or solve. A third future direction is the application of concepts from this work to the monitoring of other languages. A fourth future direction consists of further tuning the framework and integrating it with Icon compiler technology.

### 14.3.1    Update Variation in Simultaneous Animations

As detailed in the chapter on system performance, some events occur very frequently compared with others. Since graphic output is often a bottleneck in the present system, animations based on frequent events such as location changes reduce or preclude the effectiveness of animations based on less frequent events.

Mitigating the effects of this problem is an open area for research. Clearly, the faster the overall execution is, the faster the slowest animation in a group runs, but then faster animations' motion will be too fast to be useful. One possible way for monitors of frequent kinds of events to coexist with monitors of infrequent events is if the monitors of frequent events sample their events at some rate determined by the less frequently updated monitors. For EMs that do not maintain a model of TP state, this may work; for EMs such as Algae that do maintain a model, it will not. The best such EMs can hope to do is implement a reduced output mode in order to improve slower EMs' animation rates by improving overall execution speed.

In addition to motivating techniques that improve overall performance, the difference in event frequencies motivates the use of less expensive animation techniques that produce less distortion for other concurrently running EMs. For example, it is attractive to scroll an entire window a pixel at a time when running standalone, but when a monitor is run alongside other EMs, smooth scrolling distorts other EMs' animations and may cause the graphics system to fall far behind the TP execution.

## 14.3.2   Concurrency Among Monitors

Our monitoring framework is interactive and allows full debugging, unlike most event-based monitoring and debugging systems. This degree of interaction means that by design, the TP cannot continue its execution concurrently while an EM is processing an event and/or user input.

On the other hand, EMs are typically independent of one another and if MT Icon were extended to allow true concurrency on multiprocessor hardware, all the EMs interested in any given event could run concurrently. As more and better EMs are developed, the growing motivation to run more EMs more frequently will create an interest in shared memory multiprocessors.

## 14.3.3   Integrating Monitors Into Coordinators

Our framework allows EMs to be compiled and executed separately, or in conjunction with one another using an MC. Under an MC, a large number of task switches may take place with each event. Although this has not been prohibitive in practice, the possibility of merging commonly used EM functionality directly into the MC and avoiding the task switching overhead is attractive. For example, the interactive runtime error conversion and elapsed CPU time features of Eve were first implemented as standalone EMs and later added to Eve.

Less commonly used EMs can remain standalone and be loaded separately. The ability to add EM functionality into an MC is also attractive in light of Icon compiler technology discussed below, in which the MC performance may be substantially increased. Merging functionality could be accomplished relatively easily for EMs that use callbacks. EMs that utilize their own flow of control to change states from event to event would require more effort to integrate.

### 14.3.4    Integrating the Icon Interpreter and Compiler

The MT Icon facilities are specific to the Icon interpreter and are not supported by the Icon compiler [72]. On the other hand, the Icon compiler offers significant performance improvements over the interpreter. The two systems share the same runtime code and data representation, and there is no fundamental reason why an EM cannot be compiled by the Icon compiler and linked with interpreter code so that it is able to load and execute interpreted Icon programs. Since the vast majority of time spent in most monitoring situations is spent in the EM, the ability to execute EMs at compiled speeds would dramatically improve monitoring performance. This improvement could apply to monitor coordinators such as Eve without losing the flexibility of the current system, in which dynamically loaded EMs can be selected from a menu and run together under an MC.

### 14.3.5    More Execution Monitors

The purpose of the research presented in this book was to facilitate the development of new EMs. The collection of EMs implemented so far in testing the framework is in no way exhaustive. Now that the framework is implemented and has been proven useful, more EMs should be developed. As of yet, relatively few EMs provide user control over the details of the information presented. Existing EMs are oriented towards general program understanding (and particularly visualization) tasks. The development of exploratory execution monitors using this framework still has large unexplored potential. EMs that provide more specific debugging facilities have yet to be written, and have obvious utility. In addition, EMs have application areas in special contexts that have not been treated, such as the education of novice programmers.

### 14.3.6    More Types of Events; Finer Selection Controls

The event monitoring instrumentation in the present system is extensive, but in a language with as much built-in behavior as Icon, it will almost always be possible to add more types of events. For example, no instrumentation is currently available to monitor certain control structures such as alternation and limitation, to monitor the dynamic hash table activity used in Icon's built-in set and table data types, or to monitor I/O such as file and window activity.

The existing system has certain events that would benefit from further subdivision into different event codes. Conversion events might usefully be coded by destination type the way allocation events are, for example. There are other events for which finer selections than the event mask mechanism may be appropriate, similar to the selection of virtual machine instructions of interest via opmask(). Generally, these are just performance enhancements, and the current system performs satisfactorily. Nevertheless, events for which this finer selection might be useful include location events and operator and function events.

### 14.3.7   Language Support for Trapped Variables

The nonintrusive techniques for the monitoring of individual variables that are presented in Chapter 11 do not scale well when large numbers of variables need to be monitored. For such applications, data-intrusive language support for *trapped variables* would provide a better alternative.

There are two primary operations on variables that are of interest: assignments and dereferencing operations. A variable trap mechanism might insert a layer of indirection into a trapped variable reference; the intermediate block inserted between the variable descriptor and its value would cause a side effect such as an event to occur when the variable was assigned or dereferenced. Trapped variables are data-intrusive, but not problematically so, since the intermediate block might be allocated in the EM rather than the TP.

The concept of a trapped variable is old [22], and underlies such mechanisms as the SNOBOL4 variable association facility [31]. Adding trapped variable support to Icon is nontrivial but not impractical. Since the technique is complementary to the approaches presented in this book, adding it would improve the overall capabilities of the framework.

### 14.3.8   Preemptive Scheduling Monitor Coordinators

No event mask is used when Eve sends an event report to an EM; the EM runs until it requests its next event. Under some circumstances, an MC may want to regain control from an EM that consumes excessive resources by monitoring the EM, requesting event reports for clock ticks, for example. This would enable an MC to give priority to some EMs over others, or ensure that all EMs receive regular CPU time in order to handle user interaction promptly.

## 14.4    Final Thoughts

The neglect of execution monitoring in the literature makes it no surprise that no major programming language has been designed with explicit *linguistic* support (as opposed to library packages and other extralinguistic forms of support) for monitoring; such support has at best come after the fact, and is more often entirely missing. Without such support, the literature is filled with articles on how to implement crude forms of monitoring using low-level techniques and nonportable operating system and machine architecture capabilities and articles that present high-level abstractions of monitoring with no demonstration of their application to practical problems.

MT Icon represents a successful grafting of support for execution monitoring onto an existing language. Being an afterthought, its design and implementation are naturally somewhat constrained. The question arises: in a new high-level language, if support for execution monitoring is an explicit design goal, what features should be present? MT Icon suggests some of them (dynamic loading, synchronous tasks), but it may be possible to conceive of better services than MT Icon provides, and a better execution model with which to perform monitoring.

# Appendix A: Algae

This appendix presents the Icon source code for Algae, the example execution monitor introduced in Chapter 8 and enhanced in Chapters 10 and 11.

```
#######################################################
#
# File: algae.icn
#
# Subject: Program to show expression evaluation as "algae"
#
# Author: Clinton Jeffery
#
# Date: 5/1/92
#
#######################################################
#
# Press ESC or q to quit
# Left mouse assigns specific (row,column) break "points"
# Middle mouse assigns absolute depth and width break lines
# Right button erases assigned break "points"
#
# When paused due to a break, you can:
#
# c to continue
# s to single step
# C to clear one point and continue
```

```
# " " to clear everything and continue
#

$include "evdefs.icn"
link evinit
link evutils
link options
link optwindw
link hexlib
link evaltree

global scale,                       # cell (hexagon or square) size
    step,                           # single step mode
    numrows,                        # number of cell rows
    numcols,                        # number of cell columns
    spot,                           # cell−fill procedure (hex or square)
    mouse,                          # cell−mouse−locator procedure
    Visualization,                  # the window
    wHexOutline,                    # binding for drawing cell outlines
    depthbound,                     # call−depth on which to break
    breadthbound,                   # suspension−width on which to break
    hotspots                        # table of individual cells on which to break

record algae_activation(node, row, column, parent, children, color)


#
# main() − program entry point. The main loop is in evaltree().
#
procedure main(av)
    local codes, algaeoptions
    #
    # pull off algae options (don't consume child's options in this call
    # to options()).
    #
    algaeoptions := [ ]
    while av[1][1] == "−" do {
        put(algaeoptions, pop(av))
        if algaeoptions[−1] == "−f" then put(algaeoptions, pop(av))
        }
    EvInit(av) | stop("Can't EvInit ",av[1])
    codes := algae_init(algaeoptions)
    evaltree(codes, algae_callback, algae_activation)
    WAttrib("windowlabel=Algae: finished")
```

```
    EvTerm(&window)
end


#
# algae_init() — initialization and command—line processing.
# This procedure supplies default behavior and handles options.
#
procedure algae_init(algaeoptions)
    local t, position, geo, codes, i, cb, coord, e, s, x, y, m, row, column
    t := options(algaeoptions,
            winoptions() || "P:S:—geo:—square!—func!—scan!—op!—noproc!")
    /t["L"] := "Algae"
    /t["B"] := "cyan"
    scale := \t["S"] | 12
    if \t["square"] then {
        spot := square_spot
        mouse := square_mouse
        }
    else {
        scale /:= 4
        spot := hex_spot
        mouse := hex_mouse
        }
    codes := cset(E_MXevent)
    if /t["noproc"] then codes ++:= ProcMask
    if \t["scan"] then codes ++:= ScanMask
    if \t["func"] then codes ++:= FncMask
    if \t["op"] then codes ++:= OperMask
    hotspots := table()
    &window := Visualization := optwindow(t) | stop("no window")
    numrows := (WHeight() / (scale * 4))
    numcols := (WWidth() / (scale * 4))
    wHexOutline := Color("white")    # used by the hexagon library
    if /t["square"] then starthex(Color("black"))
    return codes
end


#
# algae_callback() — evaltree callback procedure for algae.
# Called for each event, it updates the screen to correspond
# to the change in the activation tree.
#
procedure algae_callback(new, old)
```

```
local coord, e
initial {
    old.row := old.parent.row := 0; old.column := old.parent.column := 1
    }
case &eventcode of {
    !CallCodes: {
        new.column := (old.children[−2].column + 1 | computeCol(old)) | stop("eh?")
        new.row := old.row + 1
        new.color := Color(&eventcode)
        spot(\old.color, old.row, old.column)
        }
    !ReturnCodes |
    !FailCodes: spot(Color("light blue"), old.row, old.column)
    !SuspendCodes |
    !ResumeCodes: spot(old.color, old.row, old.column)
    !RemoveCodes: {
        spot(Color("black"), old.row, old.column)
        WFlush(Color("black"))
        delay(100)
        spot(Color("light blue"), old.row, old.column)
        }
    E_MXevent: do1event(&eventvalue, new)
    }
spot(Color("yellow"), new.row, new.column)
coord := location(new.column, new.row)
if \step | (\breadthbound <= new.column) | (\depthbound <= new.row) |
    \ hotspots[coord] then {
    step := &null
    WAttrib("windowlabel=Algae stopped: (s)tep (c)ont ( )clear ")
    while e := Event() do
        if do1event(e, new) then break
    WAttrib("windowlabel=Algae")
    if \ hotspots[coord] then spot(Color("light blue"), new.row, new.column)
    }
end



#
# procedures for the "−square" option, display Algae using squares
# instead of hexagons.
#

# Draw a square at (row, column)
procedure square_spot(w, row, column)
```

```
    FillRectangle(w, (column − 1) * scale, (row − 1) * scale, scale, scale)
end


# encode a location value (base 1) for a given x and y pixel
procedure square_mouse(y, x)
    return location(x / scale + 1, y / scale + 1)
end

#
# clearspot() removes a "breakpoint" at (x,y)
#
procedure clearspot(spot)
    local s2, x2, y2
    hotspots[spot] := &null
    y := vertical(spot)
    x := horizontal(spot)
    every s2 := \!hotspots do {
        x2 := horizontal(s2)
        y2 := vertical(s2)
    }
    spot(Visualization, y, x)
end

#
# setspot() sets a breakpoint at (x,y) and marks it orange
#
procedure setspot(loc)
    hotspots[loc] := loc
    y := vertical(loc)
    x := horizontal(loc)
    spot(Color("orange"), y, x)
end

#
# do1event() processes a single user input event.
#
procedure do1event(e, new)
    local m, xbound, ybound, row, column, x, y, s
    case e of {
        "q" |
        "\e": stop("Program execution terminated by user request")
        "s": {                           # execute a single step
            step := 1
```

```
            return
            }
      "C": {                              # clear a single break point
          clearspot(location(new.column, new.row))
          return
          }
      " ": {                              # space character: clear all break points
          if \depthbound then {
              every y := 1 to numcols do {
                  if not who_is_at(depthbound, y, new) then
                      spot(Visualization, depthbound, y)
                  }
              }
          if \breadthbound then {
              every x := 1 to numrows do {
                  if not who_is_at(x, breadthbound, new) then
                      spot(Visualization, x, breadthbound)
                  }
              }
          every s := \!hotspots do {
              x := horizontal(s)
              y := vertical(s)
              spot(Visualization, y, x)
              }
          hotspots := table()
          depthbound := breadthbound := &null
          return
          }
      &mpress | &mdrag: {          # middle button: set bound box break lines
          if m := mouse(&y, &x) then {
              row := vertical(m)
              column := horizontal(m)
              if \depthbound then {   # erase previous bounding box, if any
                  every spot(Visualization, depthbound, 1 to breadthbound)
                  every spot(Visualization, 1 to depthbound, breadthbound)
                  }
              depthbound := row
              breadthbound := column
              #
              # draw new bounding box
              #
              every x := 1 to breadthbound do {
                  if not who_is_at(depthbound, x, new) then
                      spot(Color("orange"), depthbound, x)
```

```
                    }
            every y := 1 to depthbound − 1 do {
                if not who_is_at(y, breadthbound, new) then
                    spot(Color("orange"), y, breadthbound)
                }
            }
        }
    &lpress | &ldrag: {              # left button: toggle single cell breakpoint
        if m := mouse(&y, &x) then {
            xbound := horizontal(m)
            ybound := vertical(m)
            if hotspots[m] === m then
                clearspot(m)
            else
                setspot(m)
            }
        }
    &rpress | &rdrag: {              # right button: report node at mouse loc.
        if m := mouse(&y, &x) then {
            column := horizontal(m)
            row := vertical(m)
            if p := who_is_at(row, column, new) then
                WAttrib("windowlabel=Algae " || image(p.node))
            }
        }
    }
end

#
# who_is_at() − find the activation tree node at a given (row, column) location
#
procedure who_is_at(row, col, node)
    while node.row > 1 & \node.parent do
        node := node.parent
    return sub_who(row, col, node)     # search children
end

#
# sub_who() − recursive search for the tree node at (row, column)
#
procedure sub_who(row, column, p)
    local k
    if p.column === column & p.row === row then return p
    else {
```

```
            every k := !p.children do
                if q := sub_who(row, column, k) then return q
            }
    end


#
# computeCol() − determine the correct column for a new child of a node.
#
procedure computeCol(parent)
    local col, x, node
    node := parent
    while \node.row > 1 do            # find root
        node := \node.parent
    if node === parent then return parent.column
    if col := subcompute(node, parent.row + 1) then {
        return max(col, parent.column)
        }
    else return parent.column
end


#
# subcompute() − recursive search for the leftmost tree node at depth row
#
procedure subcompute(node, row)
    # check this level for correct depth
    if \node.row = row then return node.column + 1
    # search children from right to left
    return subcompute(node.children[*node.children to 1 by −1], row)
end


#
# Color(s) − return a binding of &window with foreground color s;
# allocate at most one binding per color.
#
procedure Color(s)
  static t, magenta
  initial {
      magenta := Clone(&window, "fg=magenta") | stop("no magenta")
      t := table()
      /t[E_Fcall] := Clone(&window, "fg=red") | stop("no red")
      /t[E_Ocall] := Clone(&window, "fg=chocolate") | stop("no chocolate")
      /t[E_Snew] := Clone(&window, "fg=purple") | stop("no purple")
      }
  if *s > 1 then
```

```
    / t[s] := Clone(&window, "fg=" || s) | stop("no ",image(s))
  else
    / t[s] := magenta
  return t[s]
end


procedure max(x,y)
    if x < y then return y else return x
end
```

Algae relies on the **evaltree** library module, which maintains the tree of currently active and suspended procedures during a monitored program's execution.

```
#######################################################
#
# Name: evaltree.icn
#
# Title: Maintain activation tree
#
# Author: Clinton Jeffery
#
# Date: July 28, 1992
#
#######################################################
#
# Usage: evaltree(cset, procedure, record constructor)
#
# Requires: MT Icon and event monitoring.
# the record type must have fields node, parent, children
#
#######################################################
#
$include "evdefs.icn"

record __evaltree_node(node,parent,children)

global CallCodes,
    SuspendCodes,
    ResumeCodes,
    ReturnCodes,
    FailCodes,
    RemoveCodes

procedure evaltree(mask, callback, activation_record)
```

```
local c, current, child, p

/activation_record := _evaltree_node
CallCodes := string(mask ** cset(E_Pcall || E_Fcall || E_Ocall || E_Snew))
SuspendCodes := string(mask ** cset(E_Psusp || E_Fsusp || E_Osusp || E_Ssusp))
ResumeCodes := string(mask **
                        cset(E_Presum || E_Fresum || E_Oresum || E_Sresum))
ReturnCodes := string(mask ** cset(E_Pret || E_Fret || E_Oret))
FailCodes := string(mask ** cset(E_Pfail || E_Ffail || E_Ofail || E_Sfail))
RemoveCodes := string(mask ** cset(E_Prem || E_Frem || E_Orem || E_Srem))

current := activation_record()
current.parent := activation_record()
current.children := []
current.parent.children := []

while EvGet(mask) do {
    case &eventcode of {
        !CallCodes: {
            c := activation_record()
            c.node := &eventvalue
            c.parent := current
            c.children := []
            put(current.children, c)
            current := c
            callback(current, current.parent)
            }
        !ReturnCodes | !FailCodes: {
            p := pull(current.parent.children)
            current := current.parent
            callback(current, p)
            }
        !SuspendCodes: {
            current := current.parent
            callback(current, current.children[−1])
            }
        !ResumeCodes: {
            current := current.children[−1]
            callback(current, current.parent)
            }
        !RemoveCodes: {
            if child := pull(current.children) then {
                while put(current.children, pop(child.children))
                callback(current, child)
```

```
            }
        else {
            if current === current.parent.children[−1] then {
                p := pull(current.parent.children)
                current := current.parent
                callback(current, p)
                next
                }
            else stop("evaltree: unknown removal")
            }
        }
    default: {
        callback(current, current)
        }
    }
}
end
```

# Appendix B: Eve

This appendix presents the Icon source code for Eve, the example monitor coordinator presented in Chapter 12.

```
###############################################################
#
# File: eve.icn
#
# Subject: Program to control multiple execution monitors
#
# Author: Clinton Jeffery
#
# Date: November 17, 1992
#
###############################################################
#
# Version: 3.2
#
###############################################################
#
# An execution monitor coordinator
#

$include "evdefs.icn"
link evutils
link options
```

```
link optwindw
link vidgets
link vbuttons
link vslider
link vstyle
link vtext
link vstopsgn

global
    cmd,                        # target program file name
    clients,                    # list of client objects
    unioncset,                  # union of client's csets
    root,                       # root of the widget tree
    msg,                        # main message widget
    enabled,                    # list of checkbox widgets
    stopSign,                   # state of the stop sign widget
    stopstate,                  # state of the stop sign widget
    EventCodeTable,             # table of EMs to call for each event
    loaded,                     # list of checkbox widgets
    delayval,                   # amount of slowdown to insert per event
    verbose,                    # switch to make Eve explain itself
    candidates,                 # list of potential EMs to run
    ticksum,                    # number of clock ticks elapsed in TP
    EveHandlers,                # Eve's procedures for each event
    EveBroadcastQueue,          # queue used for EM − EM communication
    vidget2index

global ScriptProgs


#
# main() − initializes TP, EMs, Eve's own tables, then enters the main loop
#
procedure main(av)
    local optable, all, i, aborter, monitor,
        arglist, C

    optable := parseArgs(av)
    candidates := readConfig(optable["f"], optable["all"])
    vidget2index := table()
    if /ScriptProgs then {
        cmd := pop(av) |
            stop("Eve: Icon program command−line argument is missing!")
        &eventsource := load(cmd, av) | stop("can't load ", image(cmd))
```

```
            if \verbose then
                write("Eve: Monitoring ", cmd, " (", image(&eventsource), ")")

            selectEMs(optable)
            initializeEMs(optable)

            initializeEve()
            if \verbose then write("Eve: executing monitored program")
            mainLoop()
            set_Vstrset_coupler(stopstate, , "done")
            stopsigndone(stopSign)
            drawtime()
            eveQuit()
            }
        else {
            while *ScriptProgs > 0 do {
                x := pop(ScriptProgs)
                av := pop(x)
                cmd := pop(av)
                if av[−1][1]=="<" then {
                    in := pull(av)[2:0]
                    in := open(in) | stop("can't open redirected file ", in)
                    }
                else {
                    in := &input
                    }
                &eventsource := load(cmd, av, in) | stop("can't load ", image(cmd))
                clients := [ ]
                av := pop(x)
                every i := 1 to * av do {
                    arglist := av[i]
                    put(clients, client(pop(arglist), arglist, i))
                }
                initializeEMs(optable)
                initializeEve(noop,noop)
                if \verbose then write("Eve: executing monitored program")
                mainLoop()
                write(cmd," finished")
                }
            }
    end

    procedure noop()
```

```
      end

#
# mainLoop() — Eve's main loop
#
procedure mainLoop()
    while EvGet(unioncset) do {
        #
        # Call Eve's own handler for this event, if there is one.
        #
        (\ EveHandlers[&eventcode]) ()
        #
        # Forward the event to those EMs that want it.
        #
        every monitor := !EventCodeTable[&eventcode] do
            if C := event( , , monitor.prog) then {
                if C ~=== monitor.mask then {
                    while type(C) ~== "cset" do {
                        if C === "abort" then fail
                        #
                        # The EM has raised a signal; pass it on, then
                        # return to the client to get his next event request.
                        #
                        broadcast(C, monitor)
                        if not (C := event( , , monitor.prog)) then {
                            unschedule(monitor)
                            break next
                            }
                        }
                    if monitor.mask ~===:= C then
                        computeUnionMask()
                    }
                }
            else {
                unschedule(monitor)
                }
        delay(6 < delayval)
        }
    end

#
# parseArgs() — initialize the target program
#
procedure parseArgs(av)
```

```
    local optable, eveoptions

    delayval := 0
    *av > 0 | stop("usage: eve [−f eveconfig] [−s] [−all] icon−command−line")
    #
    # pull off eve options (don't consume child's options in this call
    # to options()).
    #
    eveoptions := []
    while av[1][1] == "−" do {
        put(eveoptions, pop(av))
        if eveoptions[−1] == "−f" then put(eveoptions, pop(av))
        }
    optable := options(eveoptions, "P:V!−geo:f:s−all!")
    /optable["P"] := "0,0"
    /optable["f"] := getenv("HOME") || "/.eve"
    /optable["L"] := "Eve"
    /optable["T"] := "helvetica,bold,17"
    /optable["H"] := 100
    /optable["W"] := 100
    verbose := optable["V"]

    return optable
end

global tp,ems
#
# selectEMs − select the execution monitors
#
procedure selectEMs(optable)
    local all, i, titles, title, wantheight, maxwidth
    all := optable["all"]
    titles := getTitles()
    &window := optwindow(optable) | stop("no &window")
    maxwidth := calcWidth(titles)
    wantheight := WAttrib("fheight") * (*candidates + 1) + WAttrib("ascent")
    wantheight <:= 80
    WAttrib("width=" || (maxwidth + 101 + TextWidth("loadiconifyenable") + 16))
    WAttrib("height=" || wantheight)
    wantheight <:= 240

    # build buttons and sliders on Eve's window
    root := Vroot_frame(&window)
    attachClientControls(titles, maxwidth, all)
```

```
    VResize(root)

    # allow user to select EMs
    while(pop(Pending()))
    until stopstate.value ~=== "startup" do
        run()
    if wantheight ~= WAttrib("height") then WAttrib("height="||wantheight)
    attachSlider()
    while(pop(Pending()))
    clients := []
    every i := 1 to * candidates do
        if \all | \loaded[i].callback.value then {
            arglist := titledparse(candidates[i])
            put(clients, client(pop(arglist), arglist, i))
            }
    # the first time through we activate the clients with no useful value
end

procedure initializeEMs()
    if \verbose then write("Eve: initializing ", *clients, " clients")
    every i := 1 to *clients do
        clients[i].mask := @ clients[i].prog
end

#
# initializeEve() − initialize Eve's own state variables
#
procedure initializeEve(tickHandler,eventHandler)
    /tickHandler := eveTick
    ticksum := 0
    EveHandlers := table()
    EveHandlers[E_Tick] := tickHandler
    if /eventHandler then EveHandlers[E_MXevent] := eveEvent
    EveHandlers[E_Error] := eveError
    computeUnionMask()
end

#
# calcWidth() − compute the width needed for Eve window, in pixels
#
procedure calcWidth(titles)
    local maxwidth
    maxwidth := 0
    every maxwidth <:= TextWidth(!titles)
```

```
        maxwidth <:= TextWidth("Executing program " || cmd) + 4
        maxwidth +:= TextWidth("..")
        return maxwidth
    end


#
# getTitles() — from a list of candidates, build a list of titles
#
procedure getTitles()
    local titles, i
    titles := list(*candidates)
    every i := 1 to *candidates do
        if candidates[i][1] == "\"" then
            candidates[i] ? {
                move(1)
                titles[i] := tab(find("\""))
                }
        else
            titles[i] := candidates[i]
    return titles
end


#
# attachClientControls() — attach controls for each possible EM,
# as well as Eve's stopsign and exit button
#
procedure attachClientControls(titles,maxwidth,all)
    local fheight, y, dotwidth
    fheight := WAttrib("fheight")
    descent := WAttrib("descent")
    dotwidth := TextWidth(".")
    loaded := list(*candidates)
    enabled := list(*candidates)
    every i := 1 to *candidates do {
        y := i * fheight + descent
        title := left(titles[i], maxwidth / dotwidth, ".")
        while TextWidth(title) > maxwidth do title := left(title, *title − 1)
        Vmessage(root, 101, y, &window, title)
        loaded[i] :=
            FixedCheckbox(all, root, 101 + maxwidth, y,
                        &window, loadedChange, i, fheight)
        vidget2index[loaded[i]] := i
        xxx := FixedCheckbox(&null,root, 101 + maxwidth + TextWidth("load") + 8,
                        y, &window, iconicChange, i, fheight)
```

```
        vidget2index[xxx] := i
        enabled[i] :=
            FixedCheckbox(all, root, 101 + maxwidth + TextWidth("loadiconify") + 16,
                        y, &window, enableChange, i, fheight)
        vidget2index[enabled[i]] := i
        }

    stopstate := Vstrset_coupler(if /all then "startup" else "running",,,,,,
                            ["startup","running","stopped","done"])
    stopSign := stopsign(&window, stopstate,"stopsign",,80,80,80)
    aborter := stopsign(&window, Vstrset_coupler("abort",,,,,,,["abort"]),"aborter",,100,70,70)

    insert(Vrecset, "stopsign_rec")
    VInsert(root, stopSign, 10, 0)
    msg := Vmessage(root, 101, 0, &window, "Select client monitors")
    VInsert(root, Vline(&window, 101, fheight,
                        101 + TextWidth("Select client monitors"), fheight))
    Vmessage(root, 101 + maxwidth, 0, &window, "load")
    Vmessage(root, 101 + maxwidth + TextWidth("load") + 8, 0, &window, "iconify")
    Vmessage(root, 101 + maxwidth + TextWidth("loadiconify") + 16, 0,
        &window, "enable")
    VInsert(root, aborter, 0, 80)
end


#
# attachSlider() - attach slider for execution speed control
#
procedure attachSlider()
    VRemove(root, msg)
    Vmessage(root, 101, 0, &window, "Executing program " || cmd)
    Vvert_slider(root, 45, 180, &window, speed, , WHeight()-190, 10, 0, 100, 0)
    Vmessage(root, 10, 175, &window, "slow")
    Vmessage(root, 10, WHeight() - 20, &window, "fast")
    VResize(root)
end


#
# speed() - set the speed from the slider value. A vidget callback.
#
procedure speed(foo, newdelay)
    delayval := integer(newdelay ^ 1.5)
end


#
```

```
# run() – vidget event handler; yields control after every event by suspending
#
procedure run(e, x, y)
    local return_value

    if \e then {
        if return_value := VEvent(root, e, x, y) then suspend return_value
        else suspend
        }
    repeat {
        e := Event()
        if return_value := VEvent(root, e, &x, &y) then
            suspend return_value
        else suspend
        }
end


#
# titledparse() – parse command lines with an optional string title
# at the front. The syntax of .eve file lines is
# ["title"] cmd [options]
#
procedure titledparse(s)
    if s[1] == "\"" then
        s ? {
            move(1)
            tab(find("\""))
            move(1)
            tab(many(' '))
            return parse(tab(0))
            }
    else return parse(s)
end


#
# Trivial command line (string) argument ––> list conversion.
#
procedure parse(s)
    local l, s2
    l := []
    s ? {
        while s2 := tab(upto(' ')) do { put(l, s2) ; tab(many(' ')) }
        if *(s2 := tab(0)) > 0 then put(l, s2)
        }
```

```
        return I
end


#
# unschedule(EM) — remove EM from those that are receiving events.
#
procedure unschedule(EM)
    local newclients, monitor
    newclients := [ ]
    every monitor := !clients do {
        if monitor ~=== EM then put(newclients, monitor)
        else write("unscheduled ", image(EM.name))
        }
    clients := newclients
    computeUnionMask()
end


#
# computeUnionMask() — determine the set of events required by the
# union of all EMs —— including Eve's tick, error and user input needs
#
procedure computeUnionMask()
    static tickset
    local monitor, c
    initial tickset := cset(E_Tick || E_MXevent || E_Error)

    EventCodeTable := table()
    EventCodeTable["noop"] := ""
    EventCodeTable[E_Tick] := [ ]
    EventCodeTable[E_MXevent] := [ ]
    EventCodeTable[E_Error] := [ ]
    unioncset := tickset
    every monitor := !clients do
        if monitor.enabled === E_Enable then {
            unioncset ++:= monitor.mask
            every c := !monitor.mask do
                if c ~=== E_MXevent then {
                    /EventCodeTable[c] := [ ]
                    put(EventCodeTable[c], monitor)
                    }
            }
    if \verbose then write("Eve: union mask ", image(unioncset))
end
```

```
#
# readConfig(s) − read the .eve file and return a list containing
# its contents.
#
procedure readConfig(s, all)
    local fin, line, candidates
    candidates := [ ]
    if \s then fin := open(s) | stop("can't open ", s)
    else if not (fin := open(getenv("HOME") || "/.eve")) then {
        fin := &input
        write("Enter a list of client command lines. A blank line terminates")
        }
    while line := read(fin) do {
        if *line = 0 then next
        else if match("Monitor ",line) then {
            /ScriptProgs := [ ]
            line ? {
                ="Monitor "
                tp := parse(trim(tab(find("with"))))
                ="with"
                tab(many(' \t'))
                ems := [ ]
                while em := tab(find(",")) do {
                    put(ems,parse(em))
                    =","
                    tab(many(' \t'))
                    }
                put(ems,parse(tab(0)))
                }
            put(ScriptProgs, [tp,ems])
            }
        else
            put(candidates, line)
        }
    if fin ~=== &input then close(fin)
    return candidates
end
```

```
#
# During execution, Eve's knowledge about EMs is stored in a list of
# records of type "client_rec".
#
```

```
record client_rec(name, args, eveRow, prog, state, mask, enabled)
```

```
#
# client() — create and initialize a client_rec.
#
procedure client(args[])
    local self
    self := client_rec ! args
    if /self.name then stop("empty client?")
    self.prog := load(self.name, self.args) | stop("can't load ", image(self.name))
    variable("&eventsource", self.prog) := &current | stop("no EventSource?")
    variable("Monitored", self.prog) := &eventsource | stop("no Monitored?")
    /self.state := "Running"
    /self.mask := "
    /self.enabled := E_Enable
    return self
end


#
# eveEvent() — event handler for E_MXevent user input event.
# If the user pressed the stop sign, the stop sign changes into a green light;
# wait until the user presses the green light before continuing.
#
procedure eveEvent()
    run(&eventvalue, &x, &y)
    while stopstate.value === "stopped" do
        run()
    &eventcode := "noop"
end


#
# eveTick() — event handler for E_Tick clock tick event.
#
procedure eveTick()
    drawtime(ticksum +:= &eventvalue)
end


#
# eveError() — event handler for E_Error TP runtime error event.
#
procedure eveError()
    local w
    if keyword("error", &eventsource) = 0 then
        #
        # this error would be fatal, handle it
```

```
        #
        if w := open("Run−time error", "x",
            "font=helvetica,bold,24", "lines=10" ) then {
            write(w, "Run−time error ", image(&eventvalue))
            write(w, "File ", keyword("file", &eventsource),
                "; line ", keyword("line", &eventsource))
            write(w, keyword("errortext", &eventsource))
            write(w, "offending value: ", image(keyword("errorvalue", &eventsource)))
            writes(w, "Convert to failure? ")
            if Event(w)===("y"|"Y") then
                variable("&error", &eventsource) := 1
            }
end


#
# drawtime() − write the current elapsed TP clock time
#
procedure drawtime(val)
    /val := ticksum
    GotoXY(10, 84)
    writes(&window, "T: ", val)
end


#
# loadedChange() − vidget callback for the "loaded" buttons
#
procedure loadedChange(vidget, val)
    local arglist, i
    i := vidget2index[vidget]
    if stopstate.value === "running" then {
        if /val then {
            # trying to turn off a load while running? Sorry...
            vidget.callback.V.toggle(vidget.callback, 1)
            }
        else {
            arglist := titledparse(candidates[i])
            write("arglist:")
            every write(!arglist)
            put(clients, client(pop(arglist), arglist, i))
            enabled[i].callback.V.toggle(enabled[i].callback, i, val)
            if /enabled[i].callback.value then enabled[i].D.draw_off(enabled[i])
            else enabled[i].D.draw_on(enabled[i])
            write(image(enabled[i].callback.value), ",", clients[*clients].enabled)
            clients[*clients].mask := @ clients[*clients].prog
```

```
                computeUnionMask()
                }
            }
        else {
            enabled[i].callback.V.toggle(enabled[i].callback, i, val)
            if /enabled[i].callback.value then enabled[i].D.draw_off(enabled[i])
            else enabled[i].D.draw_on(enabled[i])
            }
    end

    #
    # enableChange() − vidget callback for the "enable" buttons.
    # Update Eve's state, and inform client of disable/enable.
    #
    procedure enableChange(vidget, val)
        local C, monitor, i
        i := vidget2index[vidget]
        if stopstate.value ~== "running" then fail
        val := if val === &null then E_Disable else E_Enable
        every monitor := !clients do {
            if monitor.eveRow === i then {
                monitor.enabled := val
                (C := event(val, , monitor.prog)) | (write("failing") & fail)
                if monitor.mask ~===:= C then
                    computeUnionMask()
                }
            }
    end

    #
    # iconicChange() − vidget callback for the "icon" buttons.
    #
    procedure iconicChange(vidget, val)
        local cl, v, v2, i
        i := vidget2index[vidget]
        val := if val === &null then "window" else "icon"
        every cl := !clients do
            if cl.eveRow === i then {
                if not (v := variable("Visualization", cl.prog)) then
                    write("Visualization: failed")
                if find("window",image(v)) then WAttrib(v,"iconic=" || val)
                else if type(v) == "list" then
                    every v2 := !v do WAttrib(v2,"iconic=" || val)
                else write("Visualization: ", type(variable("Visualization", cl.prog))|"failed")
```

```
            }
    end

    #
    # eveQuit() − TP execution completion handler
    #
    procedure eveQuit()
        local c
        if \verbose then write("Eve: Monitored program has terminated execution")
        every c := (!clients).prog do
            cofail(c)
        GetEvents(root)
    end

    #
    # broadcast() − sent event to interested EMs
    #
    procedure broadcast(x, except)
        /EveBroadcastQueue := []
        put(EveBroadcastQueue, x)
        put(EveBroadcastQueue, except)
        flush_broadcast_queue()
    end

    #
    # flush events produced during EM − EM communcation.
    # This code appears similar to Eve's main loop.
    #
    procedure flush_broadcast_queue()
        local c, C, x, except, monitor
        while *EveBroadcastQueue > 0 do {
            x := pop(EveBroadcastQueue)
            except := pop(EveBroadcastQueue) | stop("malformed broadcast queue")
            if x === "quit" then eveQuit()
            every monitor := (except ~=== !clients) do
                if C := event( , , monitor.prog) then {
                    if C ~=== monitor.mask then {
                        while type(C) ~== "cset" do {
                            #
                            # The EM has raised a signal.
                            # Pass it on to all the others except the client.
                            #
                            put(EveBroadcastQueue, C)
                            put(EveBroadcastQueue, monitor)
```

```
                    if not (C := event( , , monitor.prog)) then {
                        unschedule(monitor)
                        if \verbose then
                            write("Eve warning: broadcast of ",
                                image(&eventcode), " aborted")
                        }
                        break next
                    }
                if monitor.mask ~===:= C then
                    computeUnionMask()
                }
            }
        else {
            unschedule(monitor)
            if \verbose then
                write("Eve warning: broadcast of ",
                            image(&eventcode), " aborted")
            break
            }
        }
    end
```

# Appendix C: Event Codes

The event codes provided in the Icon runtime system are presented below. The nature and extent of this instrumentation is discussed in Chapter 6.

## C.1   Classes of Events

| | |
|---|---|
| AllocMask | Memory allocation |
| AssignMask | Assignment |
| ConvMask | Type conversion |
| FncMask | (Built-in) Function activity |
| ListMask | List operation |
| OperMask | Operator activity |
| ProcMask | Procedure activity |
| RecordMask | Record operation |
| ScanMask | String scanning |
| SetMask | Set operation |
| StructMask | Structure operation |
| TableMask | Table operation |

## C.2    Individual Events

| Code | Value | Description |
| --- | --- | --- |
| E_Aconv | input value | Conversion attempt |
| E_Alien | # bytes | Alien allocation |
| E_Aloc | line/column # | Location change (artificial) |
| E_Assign | variable name | Assignment |
| E_BlkDeAlc | # bytes | Block deallocation |
| E_Coact | co-expression | Co-expression activation |
| E_Coexpr | # bytes | Co-expression allocation |
| E_Cofail | co-expression | Co-expression failure |
| E_Collect | region number | Garbage collection |
| E_Coret | co-expression | Co-expression return |
| E_Cset | # bytes | Cset allocation |
| E_Disable | *varies* | Disable monitoring (artificial) |
| E_Enable | *varies* | Enable monitoring (artificial) |
| E_EndCollect | null | End of garbage collection |
| E_Error | error number | Run-time error |
| E_Exit | exit code | Program exit |
| E_External | # bytes | External allocation |
| E_Fcall | function | Function call |
| E_Fconv | input value | Conversion failure |
| E_Ffail | -1 | Function failure |
| E_File | # bytes | File allocation |
| E_Free | # bytes | Free region |
| E_Frem | 0 | Function suspension removal |
| E_Fresum | 0 | Function resumption |
| E_Fret | result | Function return |
| E_Fsusp | result | Function suspension |
| E_Intcall | interpreter signal | interpreter call |
| E_Integer | result | Integer value pseudo event |
| E_Intret | interpreter signal | interpreter return |
| E_Lbang | list | List generation |
| E_Lcreate | list | List creation |
| E_Lelem | # bytes | List element allocation |
| E_Lget | list | List get, same as E_Lpop |
| E_Line | line # | Line change |
| E_List | # bytes | List allocation |
| E_Loc | line/column # | Location change |

| Code | Value | Description |
|------|-------|-------------|
| E_Lpop | list | List pop, same as E_Lget |
| E_Lpull | list | List pull |
| E_Lpush | list | List push |
| E_Lput | list | List put |
| E_Lrand | list | List random reference |
| E_Lref | list | List reference |
| E_Lrgint | # bytes | Large integer allocation |
| E_Lsub | subscript | List subscript |
| E_MXevent | window event | Monitor input event |
| E_Nconv | input value | Conversion not needed |
| E_Null | null | Null value pseudo event |
| E_Ocall | operation | Operator call |
| E_Ofail | -1 | Operator failure |
| E_Opcode | operation code | Virtual-machine instruction |
| E_Orem | 0 | Operator suspension removal |
| E_Oresum | 0 | Operator resumption |
| E_Oret | result | Operator return |
| E_Osusp | result | Operator suspension |
| E_Pcall | procedure | Procedure call |
| E_Pfail | procedure | Procedure failure |
| E_Prem | procedure | Suspended procedure removal |
| E_Presum | procedure | Procedure resumption |
| E_Pret | result | Procedure return |
| E_Proc | procedure | Procedure value pseudo event |
| E_Psusp | result | Procedure suspension |
| E_Rbang | record | Record generation |
| E_Rcreate | record | Record creation |
| E_Real | # bytes | Real number allocation |
| E_Record | # bytes | Record allocation |
| E_Refresh | # bytes | Refresh allocation |
| E_Rrand | record | Record random reference |
| E_Rref | record | Record reference |
| E_Rsub | subscript | Record subscript |
| E_Sbang | set | Set generation |
| E_Sconv | output value | Conversion success |
| E_Screate | set | Set creation |
| E_Sdelete | set | Set deletion |
| E_Selem | # bytes | Set element allocation |
| E_Set | # bytes | Set allocation |

| Code | Value | Description |
|------|-------|-------------|
| E_Sfail | old subjcet | Scanning failure |
| E_Sinsert | set | Set insertion |
| E_Slots | # bytes | Hash header allocation |
| E_Smember | set | Set membership |
| E_Snew | new subject | Scanning environment creation |
| E_Spos | position | Scanning position |
| E_Srand | set | Set random reference |
| E_Srem | old subject | Scanning environment removal |
| E_Sresum | restored subject | Scanning resumption |
| E_Ssasgn | length of result | Sub-string assignment |
| E_Ssusp | current subject | Scanning suspension |
| E_Stack | stack depth | Stack depth |
| E_StrDeAlc | # bytes | String deallocation |
| E_String | # bytes | String allocation |
| E_Sval | set element | Set value |
| E_Table | # bytes | Table allocation |
| E_Tbang | table | Table generation |
| E_Tconv | example target | Conversion target |
| E_Tcreate | table | Table creation |
| E_Tdelete | table | Table deletion |
| E_Telem | # bytes | Table element allocation |
| E_TenureBlock | size | Tenure a block region |
| E_TenureString | size | Tenure a string region |
| E_Tick | # ticks | Clock tick |
| E_Tinsert | table | Table insertion |
| E_Tkey | table | Table key generation |
| E_Tmember | table | Table membership |
| E_Trand | table | Table random reference |
| E_Tref | table | Table reference |
| E_Tsub | subscript | Table subscript |
| E_Tval | table element | Table value |
| E_Tvsubs | # bytes | Substring trapped variable allocation |
| E_Tvtbl | # bytes | Table element trapped variable allocation |
| E_Value | value assigned | Value assigned |

# Appendix D: The MT Icon Implementation

Since Icon is a public domain language with an open source distribution, lots of people have modified, extended, and maintained its source code. This appendix is a guide for Icon implementors who want to know how MT Icon is implemented. This information would be useful in porting MT Icon or adding new instrumentation to the runtime system.

## D.1   Icon Interpreter Overview

The Icon interpreter version 6.0 was documented extensively in a book by Griswold and Griswold [27]. Although the implementation has changed drastically, the interpreter execution model remains as described in that book. This appendix provides a brief discussion of the interpeter's virtual machine model and the present implementation, which differs considerably from that described in the Griswold text.

### D.1.1   The Icon Virtual Machine

The Icon virtual machine is an abstract machine that is derived from the semantics of the Icon language, rather than from capabilities of real machines. The virtual machine is stack-based, and consists of over a hundred instruction codes that manage stack memory, implement control flow, and call runtime routines for Icon's primitive operations.

## D.1.2    The Interpreter Implementation

Icon's virtual machine is implemented in RTL (for RunTime Language), a variant
of C augmented to accommodate Icon-specific type information for the parameters and results of Icon's built-in functions and operators [72]. The virtual machine
instruction loop is a tiny fraction of the overall interpreter; the vast majority of the
implementation consists of code for built-in functions and operators and support
code for pervasive language features such as garbage collection.

## D.1.3    The Implementation of Co-expressions

A co-expression has its own stack for interpreter execution and its own C stack
for built-in operations. The amount of data that is present in these stacks may be
very large, and unlike Icon's other structured values, there is no way to access
data from the state of another co-expression, except by yielding control to it; co-
expressions communicate only through the results transmitted by activation, and
any side effects made to global variables.

Although co-expression activation is achieved by the execution of a virtual machine instruction, the context switch itself is a low-level context switch, written in
assembler language for the various machines on which Icon runs. This means that
in principle, co-expression switching may take place at arbitrary points in the C
language runtime system, not just at designated virtual machine instructions. MT
Icon exploits this feature to avoid a host of awkward execution monitoring techniques used in other systems such as the modification of user code to implement
breakpoints.

In addition to separate interpreter and C stacks provided by the co-expression
mechanism, programs require additional state. Co-expressions within a single
program share a global state consisting of variables, keywords, and the heap,
while separately loaded programs have separate global state including separate
sets of global variables at both the Icon and the C level.

# D.2    The MT Icon Core

The core facilities of MT Icon are not specific to monitoring. They implement
dynamic loading and support the execution of multiple Icon programs within the
Icon virtual machine. The clever part about the MT Icon core is that it was constructed mainly using existing code in the interpreter. The amount of new code
introduced by MT Icon is small. The MT Icon core is configured into the source
by adding a line containing **#define MultiThread** to the **h/define.h** file in the
Icon sources.

## D.2.1    Dynamic Loading

The existing icode loading code was adapted to support dynamic loading. Code in imain.r that traverses the icode and initializes key interpreter pointers, such as resolve(), was generalized to be callable multiple times instead of just once at program startup. The actual implementation of function load() starts in fmisc.r and calls loadicode(), in init.r.

Code to initialize the string and block regions similarly was generalized to be callable multiple times. Different programs can be loaded and initialized with different heap sizes. All programs' heaps are scrutinized whenever any program garbage collects, so that values may be safely used across programs.

## D.2.2    Program State

Every program requires separate copies of a huge number of variables that are declared as globals throughout the Icon runtime system. Not all globals must be maintained separately for each program, but most do. In addition, each program requires separate data areas for global and static variables. All these things are defined together by **struct progstate** in h/rstructs.h. A single global variable named **curpstate** points at the current program state structure, and all references to these formerly global variables are made through this pointer.

In order to avoid adding many thousands of lines of #ifdefs throughout the runtime system, macros in h/rmacros.h redefine global variables to use **curpstate** when MultiThread is defined. The issue of maintaining separate state for each program is the main maintenance headache for MT Icon. If someone adds new globals to the Icon runtime system and doesn't add them to the program state, MT Icon's illusion of separate programs is not maintained.

Programs are allocated as co-expressions with extra space for icode and for the program state. The main stacks for loaded programs are larger than for regular co-expressions. Each co-expression maintains a pointer to the program state in which it was created. Determining whether a co-expression is a main co-expression for a given program can be done by checking whether the program state is located in the memory immediately following the co-expression block itself.

```
if (((struct b_coexpr *)block)+1 ==
    (struct b_coexpr *)((struct b_coexpr *)block)- >program) ...
```

Whenever control transfers between programs, and for certain interprogram data accesses, the **curpstate** variable needs to be changed. Co-expression activation is the most common cause of this switch, but if a program called a procedure in another program, the program state would still need to switch in order for global variables to be correctly handled. The macro **ENTERPSTATE()** changes the current program state to a new program.

### D.2.3   Function Extensions

The semantics of numerous built-in functions are affected by MT Icon. Several existing functions are generalized to take an extra co-expression parameter to indicate which program to fetch data from. Other functions are added when MultiThread is defined, even some that are not specific to multitasking or multiple programs at all! These functions are to be found in fconv.r and fmisc.r

One of the more intricate parts of the MT Icon implementation is the garbage collector. References to structures may be transmitted from program to program, so the garbage collector must work across all programs. For MT Icon, the Icon runtime system was extended to support multiple, fixed-size heaps, which has become its standard memory allocation model. During the marking phase of garbage collection, in rmemmgt.r, co-expression references' program fields are visited, and when a program that hasn't been marked is found, function markprogram() is called to mark all data referenced from that program's stack, global, static, and keyword variables.

## D.3   Monitoring Support

Event monitoring support consists of built-in functions, instrumentation, and additional code in the runtime system. This support is added to the virtual machine by adding the line:

    #define EventMon

to the src/h/define.h file in the Icon sources.

### D.3.1   Instrumentation

Automatic instrumentation is provided in MT Icon by strategically inserting calls to the RTL macro EVVal(value,eventcode) at various points. EVVal() is defined in h/grttin.h, along with two variants for Icon values with different C representations. EVVal() performs the event mask test inline, discarding unwanted events with minimal impact on execution.

The calls to EVVal() pervade the runtime system code. Calls to EVVal() cannot be placed just anywhere, since they may cause a transfer to arbitrary foreign code which may cause garbage collections. Viewing multiple programs as a concurrent programming problem helps; you can't put a call to EVVal() in a critical section in the interpreter. Macro EVVal() eventually calls mt_activate() in interp.r to perform the switch to another program's co-expression from an arbitrary point in the runtime system.

## *D.3.2*   EvGet() *and* event()

The implementation of the built-in functions specific to event monitoring are located in fmonitr.r. EvGet() activates the target program to obtain an event, supplying it with a cset mask of desired event codes. EvGet() also implements E_MXevent, the code which checks for user action in the monitor window.

event() explicitly sends an event to another program. It is similar, but simpler than EvGet() since it does not need to supply an event mask.

# Appendix E: Software and Supporting Documentation

The home page for Icon at the University of Arizona is **www.cs.arizona.edu/icon**. This site includes source code and binary distributions as well as dozens of technical reports describing many aspects of the language.

The software described in this book is based on Icon Version 9.3, for which the primary reference is by Griswold and Griswold [28]. The graphics facilities used are described extensively by Griswold, Jeffery, and Townsend [29].

MT Icon, the dialect with execution monitoring support used in this book, is present in the University of Arizona Icon source distributions, but it is not enabled by default and is not present in Arizona binary distributions. To run MT Icon programs, you should obtain the Icon-2 distribution from the University of Nevada, Las Vegas. Icon-2 is described in a book by Jeffery, Mohamed, Pereda, and Parlett [36]. Icon-2 includes support for MT Icon by default, along with numerous other language extensions. The home page for Icon-2, and any erratum for this book, is **icon.cs.unlv.edu**.

MT Icon is portable but depends heavily on Icon's co-expression facilities, which are written in assembler for each platform. At present, the co-expression switch is buggy on some Icon platforms such as the DEC Alpha, and MT Icon does not run well there. I use and support MT Icon on Sun Sparc processors, as well as Intel x86 processors running Linux and Microsoft Windows. Other platforms may or may not perform correctly.

The home page for the Alamo lightweight monitor architecture can be found at **icon.cs.unlv.edu/alamo**. This page serves primarily as a repository of papers and software for the Alamo ANSI C monitor framework, a cousin to the Icon framework described in this book.

# References

[1] H. Abelson and G. J. Sussman. *Structure and Interpretation of Computer Programs*. MIT Press, Cambridge, Massachusetts, 1985.

[2] Z. Aral and I. Gertner. Non-intrusive and Interactive Profiling in Parasight. In *Proceedings of the ACM/SIGPLAN PPEALS 1988*, pages 21–30, Sept. 1988.

[3] Z. Aral and I. Gertner. High-level Debugging in Parasight. In *Proceedings of the ACM SIGPLAN/SIGOPS Workshop on Parallel and Distributed Debugging*, SIGPLAN Notices, volume 24(1), pages 151–162, Jan. 1989.

[4] R. Baecker and D. Sherman. Sorting Out Sorting (16mm film, 30 minutes). In *Proceedings of the SIGGRAPH '81 Conference*, Dallas, TX, 1981.

[5] P. Bates. Debugging Heterogeneous Distributed Systems Using Event-Based Models of Behavior. In *Proceedings of the ACM SIGPLAN/SIGOPS Workshop on Parallel and Distributed Debugging*, ACM SIGPLAN Notices, volume 24(1), pages 11–22, Jan. 1989.

[6] J. Bertin. *Semiology of Graphics*. The University of Wisconsin Press, Madison, Wisconsin, 1983.

[7] H.-D. Bocker, G. Fischer, and H. Nieper. The Enhancement of Understanding Through Visual Representations. In *CHI '86 Proceedings*, pages 44–50, June 1986.

[8] M. H. Brown. *Algorithm Animation*. ACM distinguished dissertation series. MIT Press, 1988.

[9] M. H. Brown and J. Hershberger. Color and Sound in Algorithm Animation. Technical Report 76a, Digital Systems Research Center, Aug. 1991.

[10] M. H. Brown and R. Sedgewick. A System for Algorithm Animation. *Computer Graphics*, 18(3):177–186, July 1984.

[11] B. Bruegge, T. Gottschalk, and B. Luo. A Framework for Dynamic Program Analyzers. In *OOPSLA '93 Conference Proceedings*, pages 65–82, Oct. 1993.

[12] BSD. Ptrace(2) — process trace. In *UNIX Programmer's Manual Reference Guide*. 4.2 Berkeley Software Distribution, Feb. 1983.

[13] D. D. Clark. The Structuring of Systems Using Upcalls. In *Proceedings of the Tenth ACM Symposium on Operating System Principles*, pages 171–180, Dec. 1985.

[14] A. Dewar and J. Cleary. Graphical Display of Complex Information Within a Prolog Debugger. *International Journal of Man-Machine Studies*, 25:503–521, 1986.

[15] R. Dunn. *Software Defect Removal*. McGraw-Hill Book Company, New York, 1984.

[16] I. J. P. Elshoff. A Distributed Debugger for Amoeba. In *Proceedings of the ACM SIG-PLAN/SIGOPS Workshop on Parallel and Distributed Debugging* ACM SIGPLAN Notices, volume 24(1), pages 1–10, Jan. 1989.

[17] C. W. Fraser and D. R. Hanson. A Retargetable Compiler for ANSI C. *SIGPLAN Notices*, 26(10):29–43, 1991.

[18] G. Furnas. Generalized Fisheye Views. In *CHI '86 Proceedings*, pages 16–23, June 1986.

[19] D. Garlan and E. Ilias. Low-cost, Adaptable Tool Integration Policies for Integrated Environments. In *Proceedings of the Fourth ACM SIGSOFT Symposium on Software Development Environments*, pages 1–10, Dec. 1990.

[20] M. Golan and D. R. Hanson. DUEL — A Very High-Level Debugging Language. In *Proceedings of the Winter '93 USENIX Technical Conference*, pages 107–117, San Diego, CA, Jan. 1993.

[21] A. Goldberg. *Smalltalk-80 the Interactive Programming Environment*. Addison-Wesley, Reading, Massachusetts, 1984.

[22] R. E. Griswold. *The macro implementation of SNOBOL4; a case study of machine-independent software development*. W. H. Freeman, San Francisco, 1972.

[23] R. E. Griswold. Benchmarking Version 8 of Icon. Technical Report IPD115b, Department of Computer Science, University of Arizona, Mar. 1990.

[24] R. E. Griswold. Processing Icon Event Streams. Technical Report IPD152, Department of Computer Science, University of Arizona, Dec. 1990.

[25] R. E. Griswold. Data Representation: A Case Study. *The Icon Analyst*, 11, Apr. 1992.

[26] R. E. Griswold. Views of Storage Allocation in Icon. Technical Report IPD197, Department of Computer Science, University of Arizona, June 1992.

[27] R. E. Griswold and M. T. Griswold. *The Implementation of the Icon Programming Language*. Princeton University Press, Princeton, New Jersey, 1986.

[28] R. E. Griswold and M. T. Griswold. *The Icon Programming Language,* third edition. Peer-to-Peer Communications, San Jose, California, 1997.

[29] R. E. Griswold, C. L. Jeffery, and G. M. Townsend. *Graphics Programming in Icon*. Peer-to-Peer Communications, San Jose, California, 1998.

[30] R. E. Griswold and G. M. Townsend. The Visualization of Dynamic Memory Management in the Icon Programming Language. Technical Report 89-30, Department of Computer Science, University of Arizona, Dec. 1989.

[31] D. R. Hanson. Event Associations in SNOBOL4 for Program Debugging. *Software — Practice and Experience*, 8:115–129, 1978.

[32] D. R. Hanson and J. L. Korn. A Simple and Extensible Graphical Debugger. In *Proceedings of the 1997 USENIX Technical Conference*, pages 173–184, 1997.

[33] D. R. Hanson and M. Raghavachari. A Machine Independent Debugger. *Software: Practice and Experience*, 26(7):1–24, 1996.

[34] R. R. Henry, K. Whaley, and B. Forstall. The University of Washington Illustrating Compiler. In *Proceedings of the ACM SIGPLAN '90 Conference on Programming Language Design and Implementation*, pages 223–233, White Plains, NY, June 1990.

[35] D. Huff. *How to Lie with Statistics*. Norton, New York, 1954.

[36] C. Jeffery, S. Mohamed, R. Pereda, and R. Parlett. *Programming with Icon*. IDG Books, New York, 1999.

[37] C. Jeffery, W. Zhou, K. Templer, and M. Brazell. A Lightweight Architecture for Program Execution Monitoring. In *Proceedings of the SIGPLAN/SIGSOFT Workshop on Program Analysis for Software Tools and Engineering (PASTE'98)*, SIGPLAN Notices, pages 102–131, Montreal, Canada, July 1998.

[38] B. Johnson and B. Schneiderman. Tree-maps: A space-filling approach to the visualization of hierarchical information structures. In *IEEE Visualization '91 Conference Proceedings*, pages 284–291, 1991.

[39] D. Kimelman, B. Rosenburg, and T. Roth. Strata-Various: Multi-Layer Visualization of Dynamics in Software System Behavior. In *Proceedings of IEEE Visualization '94*, 1994.

[40] W. R. Lalonde and J. R. Pugh. *Inside Smalltalk*. Prentice-Hall, Englewood Cliffs, New Jersey, 1990.

[41] J. Lamping and R. Rao. Laying out and Visualizing Large Trees Using a Hyperbolic Space. *Proceedings of ACM UIST '94*, 18(3)(3):13–14, Nov. 1994.

[42] J. R. Larus and T. Ball. Rewriting Executable Files to Measure Program Behavior. Technical Report 1083, Computer Sciences Department, University of Wisconsin – Madison, Mar. 1992.

[43] J. R. Larus and E. Schnarr. EEL: Machine-Independent Executable Editing. In *Proceedings of the ACM SIGPLAN'95 Conference on Programming Language Design and Implementation*, ACM SIGPLAN Notices, volume 30(6), pages 291–300, June 1995.

[44] M. A. Linton. The Evolution of Dbx. In *Proceedings of the Summer 1990 USENIX Conference*, pages 211–220, June 1990.

[45] R. London and R. Duisberg. Animating Programs Using Smalltalk. *IEEE Computer*, pages 61–71, Aug 1985.

[46] C. Marlin. *Coroutines (Lecture Notes in Computer Science 95)*. Springer-Verlag, Berlin, 1980.

[47] S. Masnavi. Automatic Visualization of the Dynamic Behavior of Programs by Animation of the Language Interpreter. *Proceedings of the 1990 IEEE Workshop on Visual Languages*, pages 16–21, 1990.

[48] S. Moen. Drawing Dynamic Trees. *IEEE Software*, pages 21–28, July 1990.

[49] B. A. Myers. Incense: a System for Displaying Data Structures. *Computer Graphics*, 17:115–125, July 1983.

[50] D. M. Ogle, K. Schwan, and R. Snodgrass. The Dynamic Monitoring of Distributed and Parallel Systems. Technical Report GIT-ICS-90/23, School of Information and Computer Science, Georgia Institute of Technology, Dec. 1990.

[51] R. A. Olsson, R. H. Crawford, and W. W. Ho. Dalek: A GNU, Improved Programmable Debugger. In *USENIX Summer '90 Conference*, pages 221–231. USENIX Association, June 1990.

[52] R. A. Olsson, R. H. Crawford, and W. W. Ho. A Dataflow Approach to Event-based Debugging. *Software — Practice and Experience*, 21(2):209–229, Feb. 1991.

[53] B. Plattner and J. Nievergelt. Monitoring Program Execution: A Survey. *IEEE Computer*, pages 76–93, Nov. 1981.

[54] S. P. Reiss. Graphical Program Development with the PECAN Development Systems. In P. Henderson, editor, *Proceedings of the ACM SIGSOFT/SIGPLAN Software Engineering Symposium on Practical Software Development Environments*, SIGPLAN Notices, volume 19(5), pages 30–41, Pittsburgh, Pennsylvania, May 1984.

[55] S. P. Reiss. Connecting Tools Using Message Passing in the FIELD Environment. *IEEE Software*, pages 57–66, July 1990.

[56] S. P. Reiss. Interacting with the FIELD environment. *Software — Practice and Experience*, 20:89–115, June 1990.

[57] G. G. Robertson, J. D. MacKinlay, and S. K. Card. Cone Trees: Animated 3D Visualizations of Hierarchical Information. In *Proceedings of CHI '91*, pages 189–194, New Orleans, Apr. 1991.

[58] N. A. Salingaros. Life and Complexity in Architecture from a Thermodynamic Analogy. *Physics Essays*, 10:165–173, 1997.

[59] M. Sarkar and M. H. Brown. Graphical Fisheye Views. *Communications of the ACM*, 37:73–84, 1994.

[60] D. Socha, M. L. Bailey, and D. Notkin. Voyeur: Graphical Views of Parallel Programs. In *Proceedings of the ACM SIGPLAN/SIGOPS Workshop on Parallel and Distributed Debugging* ACM SIGPLAN Notices, volume 24(1), pages 206–215, Jan. 1989.

[61] R. Sosic. Dynascope: A Tool for Program Directing. In *Proceedings of the ACM SIGPLAN '92 Conference on Programming Language Design and Implementation* SIGPLAN Notices, volume 27(7), pages 12–21, San Francisco, California, June 1992.

[62] A. Srivastava and A. Eustace. ATOM: A System for Building Customized Program Analysis Tools. In *Proceedings of the ACM SIGPLAN '94 Conference on Programming Language Design and Implementation,* SIGPLAN Notices, volume 29(6), pages 193–205, Orlando, June 1994.

[63] A. Srivastava and D. Wall. A Practical System for Intermodule Code Optimization at Link-Time. *Journal of Programming Languages,* 1(1):1–18, Mar. 1993.

[64] R. M. Stallman. *GDB, the GNU Symbolic Debugger (Version 4.4).* GNU Project, Cambridge, Massachusetts, 1992.

[65] J. Stasko, J. Domingue, M. Brown, and B. Price, editors. *Software Visualization: Programming as a Multimedia Experience.* MIT Press, Cambridge, MA, 1998.

[66] J. T. Stasko. Tango: A Framework and System for Algorithm Animation. *Computer,* pages 27–39, Sept. 1990.

[67] K. Templer and C. Jeffery. A Configurable Automatic Instrumentation Tool for ANSI C. In *Proceedings of the 13th IEEE International Conference on Automated Software Engineering (ASE'98),* Honolulu, Hawaii, Oct. 1998.

[68] A. P. Tolmach. Debugging Standard ML. Technical Report CS-TR-378-92, Department of Computer Science, Princeton University, Oct. 1992.

[69] E. Tufte. *The Visual Display of Quantitative Information.* Graphics Press, Cheshire, CT, 1983.

[70] E. Tufte. *Envisioning Information.* Graphics Press, Cheshire, CT, 1990.

[71] E. Tufte. *Visual Explanations: Images and Quantities, Evidence and Narrative.* Graphics Press, Cheshire, CT, 1997.

[72] K. W. Walker. The Implementation of an Optimizing Compiler for Icon. Technical Report 91-16, Department of Computer Science, University of Arizona, Aug. 1991.

[73] S. B. Wampler. The Control Mechanisms for Generators in Icon. Technical Report 81-18, Department of Computer Science, University of Arizona, Dec. 1981.

# Index